All things are poss_____!

Even miracles all you have to do is have faith with prayer!!!

He will never let you down all you have to do is believe!!!

Eileen & Jack

SEEKING
RAINBOW'S END

You ~~guys~~ girls

Al Shuman

All things are possible with our Savior Lord Jesus Christ!!
Even miracles all you have to do is have faith with prayer!!
He will never let you down all you have to do is believe!!

SEEKING RAINBOW'S END

A FORTUNE HUNTER'S TALE
OF RISK & REWARD

ALY BRUNER

Seeking Rainbow's End
A Fortune Hunter's Tale of Risk & Reward
Copyright © 2020 by Aly Bruner
All rights reserved.

ISBN: 978-0-578-67369-1

FIRST EDITION

CONTENTS

PRELUDE

---

*"I haven't done too bad for a kid
without a high school education."*

—Aly Bruner

UNDER THE RAINBOW

During an attempted robbery of my jewelry in 1991 at Los Angeles International Airport, I was stabbed and almost died. I needed six units of blood to stabilize my condition. The event was so traumatic that I began to suffer the effects of post-traumatic stress disorder (PTSD). So my girlfriend Nancy and I decided to leave California forever.

By 1995 we had closed my diamond business and begun a search for the perfect property, a place where we could live well for the rest of our lives. We made a list of things the perfect property would have, including a riverbank location where good hunting and fishing were available, and some acreage surrounding a comfortable log house.

We divided our journey into three trips, and my young daughters Taryn and Tawny traveled in the car with us. The first trip took us through Oregon. It's a beautiful state, but we didn't find anything we wanted. On the second trip we went to the wide-open spaces of Wyoming and Montana and still could not find the perfect place.

On the third search, we drove to Idaho and felt confident that we would find something there. The incredible thing about Idaho is that 95 percent of the state is public land consisting of huge National Forest and Bureau of Land Management parcels. Only 5 percent of the state's land is privately owned.

On the day we entered the Gem State, the skies were crystal clear and Nancy pointed to an owl sitting in a tree. "That's good luck!" At first, I wasn't so sure, because suddenly there was a cloudburst and it rained hard and steady for about five minutes. Then the skies cleared, and a huge rainbow appeared and arched over the road from left to right. As we drove under the colorful omen, I got goosebumps all over my arms and turned to Nancy and the girls. "Today we're going to find where we're going to live for the rest of our lives!"

We pulled into a small gas station in Fairfield to get some ice cream for the kids. Whenever we would stop, I would find a copy of the real estate listings and give them to Nancy to review. It was her job to match our list of wants with the available properties so we didn't waste time looking at places we wouldn't want. This time, when I handed her the flyer, a colored piece of paper dropped into her lap with a description of an exquisite property but no pictures. As she read, she turned to me with a funny little grin.

"Is this a joke? Did you put this in here?"

"No. What do you mean?"

She read me the insert that described 10.5 acres on the Salmon River with a log house, trout pond, and a guesthouse to boot. I took the flyer out of her hands and dialed the phone number. The owner answered. His name was Forrest Baker.

"Hi. My name's Aly. Saw your listing. Is your property still for sale?"

"Well, yes, it is. I put out the flyers with the insert only an hour ago."

"Forrest, how soon could we see the property?"

It took about four hours to arrive in Challis, where the population was only 750, and then we drove another seven miles north. When we found the address and I turned the vehicle into the driveway that descended toward the buildings and the river, I began to cry tears of joy. I'd been through a lot after the stabbing. The PTSD could be medicated but the beauty of this location felt like a natural remedy.

Forrest gave us a tour of his spread that far exceeded our dreamy expectations. Not only was his acreage gorgeous, the property was adjacent to three million acres of national forest.

We went into his office and sat, with Taryn and Tawny scrambling to sit in Forrest's lap as I asked him one all-important question.

"What's your best price on the property?"

The number he offered was a real bargain.

"You've got a deal. Please have your realtor write up the contract."

"Now hold on a minute, son, where do you live now?"

I described my ranch in Castro Valley, California.

"How about you, Nancy? Where were you born and raised?" he asked.

"San Francisco."

His reaction was immediate. He shook his head and said, "I can't sell you this property. It would be culture shock for you because there are no malls for you to shop in."

I couldn't believe he was turning down our offer to accept his asking price. It was a done deal, an ace in the hole. I all but pleaded, assuring him we were ready for this big move. I hoped that my hunch he'd taken a liking to my kids and Nancy would help win the day.

"I'll tell you what I'll do," he said. "You go home and think about it for thirty days. And after the thirty days if you still want this property, I'll sell it to at our agreed price. How's that sound?"

I preferred he put the agreement in writing and told him so.

"No need, Aly. My word is good."

That struck a chord. My father Alston had raised me by often repeating, "Your word is your bond, and a handshake means more than any contract you sign!" Naturally, I accepted Forrest's offer and we shook on it.

Did we wait thirty days? Heck, no. We called him every day for two weeks begging him to sell us the land right now!

He chuckled and said, "Don't worry, son, I've got buyers that will pay me more money than I agreed to sell it to you for."

What did that mean? I feared a bidding war would begin, and we were going to have to pay a lot more money than we'd agreed on. But Forrest was a man of his word. At the end of the thirty days, he sold us our dream-come-true home at the price he'd quoted, even though we had nothing in writing.

To this day Forrest and I are very close friends and I consider him an honorary second father to me.

BEGINNINGS & BIG WINS

---

*"When I wake up in the morning,
I don't wake up to go to work.*

*I wake up to go have fun.
So when I go to work,
it's not a job.*

I'm going to play the game."

—Aly Bruner

DIAMONDS ARE A MAN'S BEST FRIEND

My decision to launch my own diamond enterprise happened not because I had a vision or was so fired up with ambition that I just had to get out there and conquer the world. The twist of fate came when I asked my employer for a pay raise and he said no.

I honestly could not understand his answer. I'd worked as a salesman at Weisfields jewelry business for a couple years, had broken every sales record, and was outselling the veterans on his staff. At one point they sent me to Seattle, Washington, to learn about how to grade diamonds and to consider using me as a manager of one of the stores. I was tall, handsome, friendly, and enthusiastic. Not to mention, I had a knack for relating with people and helping them understand the true value of the glittering diamonds, necklaces, rings, and watches they wanted to purchase.

I don't remember every word that my boss spoke. I can't recall his logic. But I remember the sensation of a ship leaving a safe harbor for adventures that would surpass mere employment. I also remember every word of my response to his decision.

"I've just become your biggest nightmare," I said with conviction. I was not shy about proclaiming that I was going to make a name for myself in diamonds. No, I was not a pirate or rapscallion. I was a treasure hunter, a fortune seeker. I was about to disrupt his dominance and others with a broadside that was completely legal, and ironically, kind of humble. I would slash prices.

What I didn't mention was that I had only about $400 to get started on my new venture. Sure, I'd made good money while employed by Weisfields, but that didn't mean I had big bucks to pour into a new business. You see, I wasn't just a salesman for the jewelry. It was my responsibility to replenish the store's inventory. While reordering merchandise for our retail storefront, I made friends with the men and women on the wholesale side of things. That group of people provided an excellent education. We would discuss quality and price for an assortment of products, agree on a deal, and then once the jewelry arrived at Weisfields, my employer would mark up the prices by as much as 350 percent. That kind of profit margin can get a man to thinking. What if I could get control of those same items but undersell the competition with a mere 30/ 50 percent markup?

That sounded tempting until I realized that Weisfields was an established chain of stores that had the cash flow to pay up front for large deliveries of gorgeous diamonds and other products. My annual income for those couple of years of employment was very good for a man in his mid-twenties, but it didn't allow me to put away stacks of cash to invest in jewelry that I might not be able to sell. Who would my first clients be? How would I find a steady stream of buyers? Here was the risk I had to confront: Business success is not luck, though I've experienced my fair share of Irish shamrocks and improbable twists of fate that helped me grow financially. Success also is not how much money you have. There is one sure-fire way to reach the heights when becoming a sole proprietor: nourish relationships. It just so happened that

I was rich in that department. When I began my diamond business I basically sold out of the trunk of my car. That kept me mobile and did not demand much overhead, such as rent and utilities for an office. I already owned a car and so I did not see it as an extra expense.

Even so, after there was an attempted robbery on the doorstep of my house with a man who put a gun to my ribs, it did not take long for me to realize that I was carrying valuables that were ideal targets for thieves, which made me vulnerable. Stolen jewelry was easy to transport and trade in the black market or wherever. That's when I decided to open an office.

Here, too, security was the main issue. Not just anyone could walk through my doors and browse. I set up a by-appointment-only business and I had employees, mostly my secretary, who could keep an eye out for me while I was working with my clients. This might seem like a limitation, but it wasn't. In my waiting room I installed an antique showcase that featured jewelry I had manufactured. While meeting with one client, I knew my secretary was helping the next guy or gal make a purchase before meeting with me.

The arrangement also carried another benefit. I could help my clientele in a personal, unrushed way. Selling diamonds was personal, in a sense. The buyer was not a cold investor of a valuable commodity. Love was often the motivation for seeking diamonds. By knowing my customer's stories, we became close, and this too helped me develop relationships.

After the scare of almost being robbed, I moved into the Hayward City Center Building. The tower felt like a friendly business fortress, where I took a corner office on the seventh floor. I grossed about $56,000 in the first month. Business picked up so quickly that I soon moved to a much larger office in the same building.

My growth was fueled, to some degree, by the good men and women I met in the industry. Norman Schwartz was a diamond sales rep for Harry Winston, who at the time was one of the largest loose diamond dealers in the world and based in New York. When I had a client who wanted a 3-carat diamond, I visited Norman in a hotel room because I knew he had a very good selection of 3-carat diamonds, and I could pick out exactly what I needed. By then I'd made some money, so I whipped out $12,000 in cash to pay him.

Later, Norman approached Harry Winston, whom I have never met even to this day, to see if it was okay for him to provide me diamonds on consignment. This was great because it meant I didn't have to pay for merchandise until I'd sold it. At first, they gave me $100,000 worth of loose diamonds— diamonds that the buyer could have set in a ring or other jewelry. I did such a good job moving the diamonds that they significantly increased the amount of my consignments. That was a big shot in the arm.

Years later, when I learned Norman was dying of cancer, I remembered his generosity. Coincidentally, I also remembered that at one point he adored my secretary.

Did I make enemies? No competitor likes to be undercut in price. The jewelry store owners hated me for slashing their 350 percent markups. As the money began to pile up, and I cornered the regional market (much like Dad had mastered catching rabbits when he was a boy and selling them to the local grocery store in Winston-Salem, North Carolina), I found hundreds of eager buyers by placing advertisements in local weekly newspapers in the San Francisco-Oakland area. My prices were way below what any other jewelry stores would sell diamonds for.

By the way, the name of my company at the time was Estate Liquidators, so those advertisements also invited private parties to bring me valuables for cash. There were days when people would line up with Rolex watches, Tiffany lamps, Persian rugs, and various antiques. I was able to make deals at great bargains because one of my hobbies was visiting antique shops. Those forays taught me a lot about value and price.

The business grew so fast I could not handle everything on my own. I recruited others to hit the road to sell my merchandise throughout California. It was a win-win situation. My ambassadors and I would share the profits from their sales, and they didn't have to pay me for the goods until they made a sale. Of course, I would not make as much on those types of transactions as the ones I did myself, but that didn't matter. A sole proprietor can only be in one place at a time. By employing sales reps and encouraging them to place their own advertisements in various newspapers, business boomed.

As for the diamond trade, in the middle 1970s, a funny thing happened as I fulfilled my threat of becoming Weisfields worst nightmare. I was so successful, Harry Winston asked Norman, who had a lot of respect for my sales ability, to make me an offer. They wanted me to work for their company and would give me a substantial salary plus travel expenses.

I was flattered. I had proved my worth. And the job would remove some of the speculation (and risk) of building my own business. Some people would consider a steady, respectable income with benefits an ace in the hole.

But not me. As nice as it was to be approached, the money they offered was much less than what I was making annually at the time. And after thinking about it, declining the offer was better for Harry and Norman too. They would keep making a lot of money from my sales, and I intended to keep growing and out-performing everyone else. They could reap those rewards without having to pay me a salary or provide other benefits. This was a win-win arrangement. Why change it? All I had to do was move the merchandise. Once I did that, more diamonds and jewelry would be provided. It was a risk to me, but it was a risk I liked.

Also, there was one more important thing about the relationship with Harry Winston. He flew me to New York— all expenses paid—so that I could pick out the loose diamonds that I knew I could sell. I was truly flattered and grateful for all the help. And I loved the independence.

Even more amazing was the depth of trust that Harry, Norman, and I had developed. After purchasing product, Norman would allow me to store his loose diamonds inventory in my safe in the Hayward City Center Building. "Aly," he said, "go through the loose diamond collection and choose whatever you want on consignment."

"That's incredible," I said.

"Why? I know you won't steal from me."

The compliment moves me to this day. A lousy thief might easily have lifted $1 million from this generous man.

Yet there is no reason to steal when you know you can succeed. In one of my best years, we sold $5 million worth of diamonds.

Eventually, I changed the name of my business to A. M. Bruner Diamond Exchange. While in Hayward, I opened a new office in Santa Clara in Silicon Valley. When I left Hayward, I also opened a second office in Pleasanton, where I added furs that were tagged "Furs by Aly" to merchandise such as Italian gold chains that I'd already been selling.

The Santa Clara office was doing really well. At the end of each year I gave a generous bonus to the man I'd hired to run the place. He was a friend, so I also gave him a Jaguar as a company car and down payment money so that he could buy a house. Then one day he quit and opened his own office, stealing my staff and luring away my clientele. His actions ruined that business and destroyed our friendship. So I closed that office.

My next steps included closing my office in Pleasanton and opening a jewelry store in Danville. Right next to that store I also opened a men's Italian clothing store.

Throughout my years in the diamond business, the good times also allowed me to be a do-gooder. After moving to Idaho, we continued to help others.

For example, I helped schools and churches with costly projects, and always had a soft spot in my heart for children. On one occasion, a little girl about three years old sat on my lap one holiday when I played Santa Claus. Nancy and my daughter Taryn were Santa's helpers. I asked the girl, "What would you like Santa to bring you?"

"A pair of shoes. My feet are cold."

Her shoes had holes and the winter temperatures were in the low teens.

I held back tears as I promised the girl her wish would be granted. Before speaking to the next child in line, I turned to Nancy and she knew exactly what to do. We decided to give the little girl much more than just shoes.

In another setting, some years later, I learned that a teenaged girl refused to attend our local school because she was poor and embarrassed by her clothes. Her mother shopped at the local thrift store where community members made donations. One day the teen's classmates mocked her because she was wearing their old dresses.

"Oh my God, my mom just donated that to the thrift store!"

The poor girl was terribly embarrassed and so stopped going to school.

By working through a local church and remaining anonymous, I offered financial assistance so the girl could shop at a local retail store and buy a whole closet full of new clothes.

Was it the stories of my father's impoverished childhood, running barefoot in the snow to check his rabbit traps, that fired my compassion? I would think so. Throughout my glorious and at times hilarious exploits seeking treasure, my love of children and their tender lives never wavered.

In Idaho, Nancy noticed that a woman she knew had placed an ad in the local newspaper offering to sell precious belongings. She was surprised and so called her friend to ask, "Why are you selling your wedding rings?"

The heartbreaking response was that she needed the money to buy food for her family. Nancy and I discussed the situation and decided to invite the woman to visit us so that we could buy the jewelry. She met with Nancy in our office where a check was written. The woman accepted the payment but before she could leave, Nancy gave back the wedding rings. It took a moment for her to understand what was happening, and then she started crying and was overwhelmed with joy.

Wigs Profit

By taking a personal interest in every transaction, I learned about the needs of my audience. My rise in the industry was fast not because I depended on very rich men and women who could afford high-priced diamonds and accessories but because my price ranges were quite broad.

For example, in the 1970s, I played backgammon with a friend who owned a Dodge dealership in Hayward, California. We'd bet $1,000 a point because we enjoyed the competition and the risk, small as it was for us both back then. He was in the market for a 10-carat diamond that he wanted to buy for his beloved wife, he could afford it, and one I had bought for my store met his needs. I had it appraised by a jeweler of his choice, and with the typical retail markup the cost came to about $135,000. However, even wealthy men enjoy a discount, and since my profit margin was much smaller, I could sell him the diamond for $75,000. These days, that same item would be worth close to $1 million.

Even with my markdown, not everyone had that kind of money. So I began to manufacture lovely necklaces and bracelets that we sold in the range of $300 to $500. If they were not exactly cheap, at least they were accessible for the average buyer. Not every sale can, or should, provide a windfall. The keepsakes designed with diamonds provided steady sales and contact with a community of buyers who remained loyal. Some were eventually able to buy more expensive merchandise in my store that I would design and have manufactured.

My inspiration for the less-expensive jewelry came from my experience of selling wigs. Yes, before diamonds, this fortune hunter sold a lot of artificial hair.

But before I get to the wigs and a beauty salon my father helped finance for a friend and me, let's talk about failure.

Due to my avid interest in cars during and after high school, I'd worked with Firestone, Big O Tire, and Goodyear, all of whom specialized in tires and wheels. Although my initial responsibilities focused on installation—I was lightning fast—I soon became adept at the up-sell of other products, such as brakes, shock absorbers, and tie rods, which made more money for the store.

One day, I was approached by a guy who owned a diesel truck that had a blown motor. If I was willing to pitch in some money to get it rebuilt, he said we could partner in a small trucking business.

I was green at nineteen years old, but a little bit shrewd with a taste for risk. I went to Wells Fargo, where my father banked, and requested a $2,200 loan for the motor repair. The money was granted. Although I had no financial track record then, my father's reputation was solid. He'd done a lot of business with the bank as a used-car dealer and real estate investor. He eventually bought a fine parcel of land in Clearlake, California, and built a sub-division with streets named after me and my sisters. "Son," he'd told me many times, "when you get some money of your own, put it in property."

"Why, Dad?" I asked.

"Because they're not making any more land."

It was one of the most lasting impressions he made on my young, malleable mind. Supply and demand. Never forget it.

Anyway, after I naively paid to have the engine fixed, my trucking partner reneged on our deal and never paid me a penny. When I revealed the situation to Dad, he was furious that the bank had loaned me money. He had a few words for me, too. Dad had no intention of covering my bum deal. I therefore worked my tail off at the tire shop to pay back every dollar. Unlike my so-called trucking partner, I'd been taught that a handshake is my bond. I was always good for the money, one way or the other.

The tire job may have seemed like typical blue collar labor, but in truth it taught me valuable lessons, such as providing a product that consumers must regularly upgrade. This just happened to mesh well with another one of Dad's philosophies: Always look for opportunity.

That idea guided me when I partnered with a friend named Jim to open the beauty salon I mentioned earlier. Our clients could have their hair washed, trimmed, coiffed, or dyed. Yet that type of business, while lucrative, had limits set by the hours we were open and the number of chairs and appointments available on any day. The one thing we didn't have was a product that might help women whose hair was damaged or did not provide a style the client wanted. A wig meant you could become a blonde or redhead with the ease of changing hats. A wig could fulfill a need.

Wigs also could be sold without limit, in theory, anyway. After successfully selling wigs to my retail clients in the shop, I began to distribute them wholesale throughout the region to other beauty salons. We got the wigs at such a good price we could sell a load of them for a decent profit. It didn't hurt that even at the ripe young age of twenty, I could be charming and enthusiastic. The salon proprietors adored my bright blue eyes and friendliness. Those qualities paved the way to bigger ventures and profits.

Eventually, our success attracted a buyer, in part because we had a terrific long-term lease at an excellent location. Also, it was a turnkey business that would allow the new owner to step right in and take over. My friend and I paid back the seed money Dad had provided and made some decent cash for ourselves, though by no means a fortune.

BIG WINS

I have been very fortunate to have experienced many big wins in my life. Was it luck? I believe good fortune happens when a person is willing to take some risks in search of treasure. I don't focus on winning. Instead, I keep an eye out for exceptional value at an excellent price.

Years ago, I was at a coin-operated and antique advertising show when a man walked in with a priceless Topsy Smoking Tobacco sign made from paper. He had bought it at a garage sale for $125 and sold it to a dealer I knew at the show for $3,600. A nice payday for the man.

But I bought the antique at the same show from Larry, the dealer, for $10,000. Was I nuts? Maybe. But I had a plan. I kept the sign for a while after doing some restoration on it. Then I sent it to an antique advertising auction in the east, and it sold for $62,500. All three sales were profitable. The catch that made it all happen was the $125 purchase at the garage sale. The buyer knew he had found a good value.

But sometimes my wins created resentments.

Not only had I purchased the Topsy Smoking Tobacco sign from Larry, I'd also agreed to partner with him to buy a group of slot machines. These were not the huge type you find in Las Vegas. I loved the Watling Rol-A-Top Coin Front 10-cent slot machines because they were smaller, only 26" tall x 15 1/2" wide x 15" deep, even though each is very heavy and requires its own stand. My investment was $25,000 and we enjoyed a handsome profit from the sale. That's when I learned that Larry didn't want to pay me my share. He was upset that

I'd made so much money selling the Topsy Smoking Tobacco. He realized he'd let me have it for a price that was way too low, and therefore, since I'd made plenty of profit from that transaction, he decided he did not owe me anything from the slot machine deal.

Nonsense.

Although I tried to reason with him, in the end I was forced to take him to court. The judge ruled in my favor, and I was awarded not only my $25,000 investment and profit share, but also half the profit Larry had made on the sale.

When I was liquidating a lot of pieces from my collection as Nancy and I planned a move to Idaho, there were plenty of bargains out there. Then the billionaire class got involved and the entire environment changed. Bidding wars between the big-money types made prices skyrocket, often out of reach even for the millionaires who loved antiques but also had a keen eye for value. In real estate, it is often said that you make money on the buy not the sell of the property. The same is true of other assets. I made a nice profit on Topsy Smoking Tobacco because the buy side was so good.

Here's a revealing example of the inflation caused by billionaires, and to be fair, other economic conditions over the last two or three decades. The assets that I liquidated for about $500,000 thirty years ago would be worth about $10 million in today's market.

Another example is the Hilda Clark Coca-Cola oval tin sign. The beautiful American model and actress became famous as the first woman to be featured by the beverage company on signs and tin serving trays. As I was liquidating my collection, the Hilda Clark oval tin signs could be purchased for about $5,000, on average. Then I found a gem that did not require restoration, so I readily agreed to pay $10,000. Most people would agree that I made a nice profit when I sold it for $16,000. But then in 2017 that same item sold for about $87,000. Advertising calendars usually don't sell for as much as metal signs, but in August, 2014, a 1900 Coca-Cola calendar in near-mint condition sold for a world record of $210,000, another indication that billionaires are still in the game and they don't care what price they pay.

Another example of outrageous pricing is a gorgeous antique by Caille Bros. Co. Roulette that I bought for $25,000 and sold for $30,000. Recently, one like it was won by the highest bidder at $330,000. I can certainly understand why someone would fall in love with it. The piece is a roulette wheel contained in a slot machine that sits on the floor like a fine cabinet. After you put a coin in and crank the handle, it works just like a roulette wheel at any casino, and it had a glass top that was flat so you could see the ball go round and round. I must say it was one of my favorite coin-operated machines.

Understanding value is a curious talent. The knowledge I gained from my own experiences helped. From a young age I loved to visit antique shops looking for bargains for my own home. But I believe the successful buyer may also have a sixth sense about quality.

For example, I bought a very rare penny arcade shooting gallery machine for $6,500 in England. That was a bargain price because there were only two known to exist in the world.

Once again, my move to Idaho prompted me to sell the unique piece. I offered it to an antique dealer and auctioneer for $10,000. He counter-offered with $7,000, which really pissed me off, so I called a penny arcade collector in the Chicago area and offered it to him for $40,000.

Frankly, my asking price was somewhat outrageous. But did the man make a counteroffer? No. He gave me my price because he was excited to have the opportunity to buy it. He understood its value, both emotionally and in the realm of the antique collector. Later, I went back to the man who had low-balled me and told him how much I'd sold it for. He nearly wept when he realized how foolish he had been.

There is value everywhere, if the fortune hunter is willing to seek diamonds in the rough and ask questions. That's why my wife, Nancy, who was my girlfriend at the time, enjoyed our trips to Butterfields & Butterfields Auctioneers in San Francisco. We would go to the warehouse sales where we found real bargains on a regular basis.

On one occasion, Nancy was paging through a B & B catalogue when she saw the name Picasso and a listing for two copper etching plates. Although they were listed, they were not in plain sight. So I went to one of the staff members and inquired about them.

"They're in a cabinet, sir."

That made no sense. A nice display of the two Picasso copper etching plates would have attracted a lot of attention. I asked if it was possible to see them before the auction started.

"Of course."

The two Picasso copper etching plates were not only in the cabinet, but they were placed in a large protective folder.

Again, I thought this was a ridiculous way to share the Spanish artist's art, but I also realized their mistake was our advantage. Seeing the two Picasso copper etching plates gave us a thrill. I was salivating I wanted them so badly. But I held my tongue.

When the auction began, Nancy and I bid $325 and waited for a hungry buyer to raise the stakes. Silence. No one else wanted the work, in part, I assume, because other buyers had not bothered to take a close look. In any case, we went home with the Picassos. But we didn't intend to hide them away.

Our next step was to contact a gallery in Vail, Colorado, that had sold my bronze sculptures of musicians that I was inspired to create in the 1990s. When I told them about the Picasso copper etching plates, they agreed to take them on consignment. Thanks to their contacts and knowledge, the two Picasso copper etching plates sold for $27,500. Naturally, they took a generous cut of that sales price, but we still got $15,000.

After we moved to Idaho and had liquidated a lot of belongings, I saw a grasshopper weathervane for sale on the Internet. I love weathervanes. The seller wanted $6,500 but we only had about $8,500 in our bank account. The money we made on sales was invested and therefore not liquid. But once again, when I want something badly, I find a way to have it.

"Hey, Nancy..."

I barely finished my pitch before she cut me off. We'd agreed to live on a shoestring for a while until we settled in our new home. "If you buy it, we'll only have a couple thousand dollars left. No."

I knew in my heart that I could make a big killing on the antique. I was not the only person in the world, after all, who adored these things. I snatched it up, then quickly contacted a collector I knew in the East. I sent him pictures and my asking price. He bought it without hesitation and planned to fly out to Idaho to pick it up. That's when I told Nancy about the whole caper.

"Guess how much I sold it for?"

"Hm. I hope you got...well...did you get as much as $10,000?"

"No, unfortunately, I didn't get anywhere near that."

"Don't tell me you took a loss!"

I love jerking her chain, now and then. I pulled out the receipt for the sale and she was stunned.

"Sorry. I could only get $50,000," I grinned.

MY FATHER ALSTON

My father Alston faced some steep challenges as a boy. When he was nine years old and in the fourth grade, his mother, my grandmother, was having an affair with a nineteen-year-old man who lived down the road on an adjoining farm. My grandfather came home and found them together. She shot her husband with a 32-caliber Smith and Wesson. She was indicted, however, they let her off because she claimed the killing was self-defense.

Shortly thereafter, Dad's mother married an old man in the area and abandoned her children. The brothers and sisters survived by eating the food from the farm, occasionally making peach and apple pies. Sometimes the pies were all that they had to eat.

More hard times followed when Dad's oldest brother, Wendell, took the tobacco crop that had taken a year to grow and dry to the marketplace and never returned with money from the sale. As a result, his other two brothers Roy and Tab and his three sisters Doodle, Beanie, and Joyce had to abandon the farm to find a way to survive on their own.

Dad at ten years old went to work at another farm nearby where he turned the soil by day and slept in the barn at night. At eleven years old he went to yet another farm, where he also took up residence in the barn, and basically provided slave labor at 25 cents a day. He convinced the owner to allow him to plant a watermelon patch with the promise that they would share the profit.

There are not enough good words in the dictionary to describe what an incredible, one-of-a-kind man my father was. He shared many stories with me through the years, though I'm sure he didn't tell me everything. It's my impression that he carried a lot of baggage that was too painful to share with me and my sister. This is what I know.

Born in 1925 in Winston-Salem, North Carolina, he was the fifth youngest of seven children. He lived to be ninety-three years old.

He grew up in hard times and didn't have much in the way of material possessions. He wore shoes that were too small, so he cut out the top front section. When he pulled on the footwear, his toes jutted out past the soles. His school clothes were no better. They were riddled with holes and he suffered physical discomfort from the boils on his fanny.

It was very difficult in those days to make money, especially for a boy. Determined to make a buck, he learned how to build traps that are called rabbit gums. They were a simple but very clever design. With scrap wood Dad would build a long rectangular box leaving one end open. Then he would fabricate and install a sliding trap door at the open end. All that was left to do was to drill a hole in the top of the box towards the rear where it was dark. That's where he would insert the trip lever that was connected to the sliding trap door in the front. The concept was also simple and clever: a rabbit would run into the dark tunnel-like box for safety. When its body hit the trip lever, the door would slide shut.

When I was nine years old and living at our home in Castlewood Country Club near Pleasanton, California, Dad made a trap for me after we noticed a rabbit hopping around the backyard hillside. It only took him about thirty minutes to build. Once it was completed, we took it up the hillside to the area where we'd last seen the rabbit. Wahoo! It worked! The next day we found the rabbit in the hand-made box.

Back to Dad's story, he gathered enough material to build one or two rabbit gums so that he could start to make money. Every day after school he would run home to check his traps. He was rarely disappointed. He would sell the rabbits he caught to the country grocery store in town. The proprietor would give him 10 cents for a small rabbit and 15 cents for a large rabbit. Alston was in business. That was when the little entrepreneur learned the value of a dollar and how to earn more.

Alston was unlike all the other kids in school. Instead of buying candy or ice cream with his earnings, he invested his money to buy materials for building more traps. During the winter months with snow and ice on the ground he would have to check his traps barefoot because he didn't own boots. Running as fast as he could from trap to trap, he would check for rabbits every day. From that point on he always had a bankroll in his pocket. He would never again run out of money.

Not that he didn't have competitors. There were other kids at school who also had a few rabbit gums, but he noticed that they weren't prosperous. When he would see them at the country store, most times they had no money and always wanted candy or ice cream. Always one to capitalize on opportunity, Alston made his short-sighted peers an offer.

After buying out the competition, he had a monopoly on the rabbit business. This was the beginning of his empire. As time went by, he eventually had forty-seven rabbit gums, more than anybody else in town.

So many childhood stories reveal his savvy, even at a young age. One of the coolest things he ever did was change the rules of a playground baseball game. The kid who owned the only bat and ball was a bully and wouldn't let Alston play. With his bankroll in his pocket from his rabbit sales, he calmly approached the bully to give him a lesson in negotiating.

"How much money would you take for that bat and ball?"

The bully responded with a ridiculous price that was more than new bat and ball would cost. No problem. Alston whipped out the cash and paid him. Then he grabbed the bat and ball and with a big grin proclaimed, "Now that's my bat and ball so you can't play anymore."

I believe that was the only time Dad intentionally overpaid for anything. But lesson learned: He got the best end of the deal!

As I came of age, Alston revealed more about his business dealings as a young man. After the Great Depression, he owned a pickup truck, but fuel was rationed as America revved up to join World War II, so people in his community couldn't travel far to buy the goods and appliances they needed. He saw that as an opportunity.

Alston took the risk to fill up his gas tank—a big expense — and drive out-of-state to buy as many refrigerators as he could possibly haul. When he got back to his town, he would set up shop on a street corner with a sign announcing, "Refrigerators for Sale."

Within a few hours he would sell everything he had hauled and for a very handsome profit. With his pockets full, he had enough money to go back for another truckload. It is one thing to see an opportunity. Dad always figured out how to capitalize on it.

During World War II while working on a construction site, Dad fell from a high elevation and crushed his ankle. That kept him out of the military. Yet had he served in Europe or elsewhere, I've got to believe he would have figured out how to make a fortune.

As his only son, I wanted to make my dad proud, but I had big shoes to fill. One of the most important lessons I learned from him was that a man's word is his bond. If you shake hands on a deal, it is better than any contract you would sign.

Now that you have passed away, I hope I have made you proud, Dad. I will love and miss you always.

MAKING MONEY WHEN I WAS YOUNG

When I was young, I was very ambitious about making my own money. In sixth grade I went to the bus depot and bought penny bubblegum and candy bars to sell at school.

I also went to the Rexall drug store in town to buy cinnamon oil so that I could make cinnamon toothpicks. I was told by the druggist at the Rexall drug store that a prescription was required to buy cinnamon oil.

"But all I want to do is make cinnamon toothpicks to sell to the kids at school. They love the taste."

I opened my bag to show the man my supply of wooden picks and he smiled.

"Clever boy," he said and then sold me the cinnamon oil.

At school I tripled my money by selling the penny bubblegum for three cents each. My price for candy bars was doubled for my investment. At ten for five cents the cinnamon toothpicks were very popular. But my success created a problem I wasn't expecting.

Dad got a phone call from the school principal who expressed concern that my peers were using their milk money to buy my bubblegum, candy bars, and cinnamon sticks.

"That's unfortunate," my dad said. "But I have to give my boy top honors for being entrepreneurial."

The principal couldn't disagree.

I was disappointed that my first venture was shut down. It seemed very unfair at the time. But knowing my dad was proud of me was a reward like no other. It put a fire in my belly to dream bigger and start new businesses.

When I was nine years old, we lived at Castlewood Country Club above the twelfth green on the golf course. I made a lot of money every year collecting golf balls that players had whacked out of bounds and then couldn't find in the weeds, or maybe they gave up the search for fear of getting a rash from exposure to poison oak. They were wiser than I was. I can't count the times I had an allergic reaction to the poison oak that made me itch like crazy. It was a painful price to pay for scooping golf balls out of bounds. But the profit was worth it.

When I was twelve years old, Dad allowed my two sisters and me to attend livestock auctions. He gave us each a paddle to raise so that we could bid on Shetland ponies. The winning bid brought us Jellybean. He earned the name because he would follow you anywhere if you showed him a jellybean.

At the time, we were living at the Bonnie Doone estate. The grounds included a huge farmhouse. It was big enough to welcome a Shetland pony. That was good because one day Jellybean was so eager to nibble on sweets that he followed me into our home. He even accompanied me upstairs to the game room. That's when Mom came home. Boy, was I in trouble!

The Shetland pony I bought for myself I named Pinto because that's what he was: a two-toned, black and white, wild mount who had not been broken. I was proud of the job I did training him.

Dad boarded horses—more than fifty— and our property included an arena where they could be shown. When Pinto was finally trained properly, one of Dad's clients came over and asked me if he could buy it for his daughter. Eager to make my father proud, I agreed to sell my Shetland pony for hundreds of dollars. What a success.

But my celebration changed to grief after I found Dad and showed him the huge check.

"You did very well, son."

"Thanks, Dad."

"However, where's your pony now?"

I immediately started crying. I'd made a handsome profit, that was for sure. But my beloved pony was gone forever.

Growing up brought new ways to make money. During golf tournaments, I'd caddy at the local golf clubs. Sometimes I would be a spotter, which meant it was my job to show the golfer where his golf ball had fallen out of bounds after he'd teed off. But the job was not without its challenges. One day, out in the sun too long, I suffered heat stroke and could not fulfill my duties. The golf pro paid me anyway. His kindness was one more lesson on my way to developing my business skills.

Always on the lookout for opportunity, I found a unique proposition in my high school's woodshop class. Often put in charge of the class by my teacher who appreciated my skills, I discovered a generous supply of black walnut wood that the school provided students free of charge so that they could build their projects. I had a better idea. I used the beautiful wood to make bowls on the lathe, and then I sold those creations at a hefty price to teachers and anybody else who wanted them.

The bowls did so well that I began to make cutting boards from ash and mahogany. Since I didn't pay a dime for the wood, my profit was handsome. It worked quite well until my teacher went to the storage area to retrieve wood for class and realized it had all been pilfered.

One of the most memorable moments in my young life happened after working at Bonnie Doone cleaning the stalls where the horses were boarded. I was so filthy, I needed a good, hot shower. When I realized my sister was using the upstairs bathroom in the farmhouse, I scooted downstairs. I knew Mom and Dad weren't at home, so I could use their private shower.

While lathering up, I heard a voice yell out, "Here I come, Honey." A moment later my stepmom Joni jumped into the shower with me. I yelped, "Mom, what are you doing in here?"

She was a very short 5'2" compared to my height that had already climbed past 6". I'd certainly never seen her naked and noticed for the first time that her entire body was covered in freckles, head to toe. "Mom!"

She didn't say a word. She just looked up at me baffled that I wasn't Dad. Then she jumped out of the shower and ran through the bedroom to find some clothes. Later, I learned that she had never jumped in with my father before. It was meant to be a surprise. And it was.

MY BIRTHPLACE AND WICKED
BOYHOOD CRIME

I was born in 1949, in Winston-Salem, North Carolina. My father's name was Alston and my mother's name was Mazie and I had a little sister in diapers named Candy. We would visit my grandparents' tobacco farm that had a lot of old-time charm. The farmhouse was shielded by big shade trees, and in the back, there was a peach and apple orchard. Across the dirt road in front of the house there was a corn crib, a barn, and tobacco fields with Pilot Mountain in the distance.

Dad was working the tobacco market back then. He'd buy a stack, then re-stack it to make it more presentable by putting the pretty stuff on top and the bad stuff underneath. By doing so he'd get 20 to 30 cents more per pound. As a result, his family did not do without. For a time, that tobacco was a good living.

Back then we were considered Tar Heels. Everyone spoke with a heavy southern accent in that part of the country and they always seemed to be speaking in slow-motion. I had six aunts and uncles on my father's side of the family and a few cousins. But I don't remember much about relatives on Mom's side.

When I was between four and five years old, my Uncle Delmo would occasionally come over to go target practicing with me using his Remington 22 semi-automatic rifle. I was not strong enough to hold the rifle on my own, so we set up a sandbag that I could rest the rifle on. I was a natural marksman shooting tin cans. I seldom missed.

One day Uncle Delmo and I were sitting on the back porch when a sparrow flew into one of the tall trees. He said, "Watch this." Raising his rifle quickly, he took a bead on the sparrow.

I yelled, "Don't shoot him!"

The rifle fired and the sparrow fell to the ground. I couldn't believe my eyes. Immediately crying, I ran over to pick up the little bird. I was appalled. He was still alive, but his beak had been shot off.

Sobbing and furious, I shouted, "How could you do that? Why, why, why did you shoot him?" I couldn't understand how my uncle could be so cruel.

Since the sparrow was suffering, uncle Delmo threw it on the ground and shot it to end its misery. It was the first thing I had ever seen killed. Realizing he had made a big mistake, he tried to distract me by setting up some more tin cans for me to shoot. I went from sorrow to anger, never wanting to see my uncle again.

I got a shovel out of the tool shed and buried the sparrow under the tree where he had fallen. I never said a word to anyone, not even my dad.

A few weeks later, my uncle showed up at the doorstep with a brand-new BB gun trying to make amends. The death of the sparrow still pained me, so I had a hard time accepting the gift. Finally, I reached for it, because it was too irresistible for a boy.

After loading the-lever action rifle with BBs, Uncle Delmo showed me how to cock it, but at first, I wasn't strong enough to do it on my own. Fortunately, it was lighter than my uncle's Remington 22, so I eventually learned to shoot BBs without resting it on a sandbag. It didn't take long before I was knocking off tin cans at 25 yards. One after another—bing, bing, bing.

My father didn't want me to keep the BB gun. But Delmo convinced him that it was a gift. Even so, Dad put it in a locked closet.

"Son, you can only use the BB gun with adult supervision. Understand?"

I nodded and for a time I obeyed. Although Alston was a busy man wheeling and dealing, he often took time to go plinking with me so that I could learn more about the BB gun. I was very proud that I was an excellent marksman and Dad was impressed, which pleased me even more because he wasn't much for compliments. One day, though, he looked me straight in the eye and said, "Son, you're a mighty fine shot." To this day it's a memory I still cherish.

It didn't take long before I figured out how to cock the BB gun on my own. Putting the tip of the barrel straight down into the ground and with both hands using all my weight, I was finally able to get the job done.

I also knew where the key to the locked closet was kept, so I began sneaking the BB gun out and practicing behind the barn. In memory of the poor sparrow, I took my anger toward my uncle out on the tin cans. Shot after shot after shot my anger grew stronger and stronger.

The target practice was fun and easy. The hard part was sneaking the rifle back into the closet. I'd peek into the window of our home and wait until the coast was clear. Then I would tippy toe back in the house to put it away under lock and key.

Weeks went by and then finally one day Uncle Delmo visited again. Right off the bat he could see the tension in me and the animosity I had toward him. Wanting to break the ice he suggested we go target practicing. My first thought was no. But I held my tongue as my blood pressure went up through the roof and devious thoughts came into my mind. With a grin on my face I responded, "Okay. Let's go."

It was a hot day and my uncle wore thin cotton shorts. I was in my standard attire—denim overalls and barefoot. Behind the barn, uncle Delmo started setting up tin cans on the fence, as usual. I grinned. Poor Uncle Delmo didn't know that I had learned how to cock the BB gun and that I intended to take revenge on behalf of the sparrow.

Bull's-eye!

The BB hit its mark on the left cheek of Uncle Delmo's ass. He let out a big yell, thinking he'd been stung by one of the yellow-jacket bees that buzzed around the barn. He jumped around and smacked his butt trying to dampen the pain, full knowing that yellow jackets don't lose their stinger like honeybees so they can keep attacking.

I quickly re-cocked and took aim at the other cheek.

Bull's-eye!

But this time he heard the BB gun fire. Pfft. He turned and saw me aiming at him. This time when he touched his butt, he discovered blood seeping through his shorts.

Busted, I lowered the BB gun and grinned. He ran to me and jerked the rifle out of my hands.

"What were you thinking?" Uncle Delmo yelled.

My grin was replaced by a serious poker face. This time I used words to wound him.

"Now you know how it feels to be shot twice! You're alive, but that little sparrow wasn't so lucky, was he?"

By the look on his face it was clear he understood exactly what I was talking about. He nodded his head at me with approval as if to indicate what just transpired was justified.

As we walked back to the farmhouse, he held my hand for the first time ever. I still can't believe what he said next. "Aly, not a word about this to anyone. It'll be just between you and me."

Dad hadn't gotten home from working at the tobacco warehouse yet and the babysitter was the only adult in the house. In the rural areas back then, farmers only went to the hospital when it was life or death. It was common practice for the lady of the house—in this case, the babysitter— to be handy enough with a needle and thread to sew up a wound, when necessary.

I can still see Uncle Delmo remove his shorts, place his hands on the kitchen table, then stand spread eagle without ever fully explaining to the babysitter how the wounds had happened. Laughing, she assumed he had slipped and fallen on a board with a couple of nails.

Pouring moonshine into uncle Delmo's butt wounds, the babysitter threaded her needle and was ready to sew him up. But he had another idea. In that part of the country, moonshine was a big business and better than store-bought whiskey. Dad's specialty was making peach brandy from our orchard. My uncle took a few healthy swigs of the hard stuff, then spoke to his surgeon.

"Grab that pair of needle-nose pliers and dig out the BBs," he said.

"BBs? What happened?"

You couldn't blame the woman for asking a sensible question. But uncle Delmo said, "Don't ask."

After dipping the pliers in moonshine to sanitize her instrument, she began to dig. Listening to my uncle's screams as she explored the BB holes created by my sharpshooting made me sick to my stomach. Only then did I feel guilty for what I had done and wished I could take it all back.

It took about half an hour to patch him up. He had downed about a quart of moonshine to soothe the pain but was still coherent enough to tell the babysitter, "Not a word of this to Alston."

I was expecting severe punishment for what I had done, but decades later the incident remained our secret. Not that I didn't indirectly receive some punishment.

One afternoon, I made the mistake of letting Dad see me cock the BB gun by myself. He made up his mind that I was too young to have a BB gun, so he concocted a story telling me that the Big Bad Wolf had come into the house and run away with the rifle. I didn't want to believe him, so I stole the key and unlocked the closet. The rifle was gone. I searched the entire house, methodically going through every square inch of every room. I even looked underneath the mattresses to see if the BB gun was there. The living room was the last room

I checked. Sure enough, there it was hidden underneath the sofa. Big mistake, Dad, I thought.

I should have kept my mouth shut, because after my father got home that evening and realized I had found the hiding place, the BB gun disappeared again. This time, forever.

GETTING IN TROUBLE CUTTING SCHOOL

When I was in high school, I had a brilliant idea that would allow me to cut class on a regular basis. In those days, if you missed school you had to have an excuse for your absence. That meant bringing in a note from your parents explaining why you had not attended. In my case, the notes always said that I was "sick" and therefore had to stay at home.

My girlfriend had gorgeous handwriting. Her skill and artistry looked like the work of a mature person. If she wrote excuse notes for me and signed them, I was convinced the principal and my teachers would believe they were authentic. That meant I could skip school whenever I wanted to go hunting and fishing with my friends.

The forgeries worked well until one day the principal grew concerned about my health. He called my parents to inquire why I was missing so much school. The call must have come as a big surprise. I imagine Mom answering, bewildered.

"Aly? Sick? He looks fine to me."

The principal asked my parents to meet him in his office, and they dragged me along with them. It felt like an inquisition. I squirmed as the principal laid out his case against me. I tried to duck some questions, but I knew it was useless when the principal reached into his desk drawer and pulled out a big stack of notes with pretty handwriting. I could feel the heat rise in my face, and I am sure I turned beet red. I was busted.

My parents examined the evidence against me, sighed, and then the principal, my executioner, expressed the obvious.

"I'm sorry, Mr. and Mrs. Bruner, but I can't tolerate this kind of behavior. I'm going to have to suspend Aly from school."

My father, a wise man, objected. He must have noticed my face brighten.

"No, sir. You're not going to suspend Aly because that's exactly what he wants."

Dad proceeded to outline a unique form of discipline that truly made me despair. He suggested that I show up at school each day, but not for class. Instead, as punishment, I would work all day helping the custodian mop the floors, clean the student toilets, and empty garbage cans around the campus.

The principal readily agreed. A deal was struck.

My penalty lasted one full week, and it was humiliating. Throughout each day, all the kids mocked and made fun of me while I did my chores.

But I won honors from a few friends. If only you could have seen their faces when I explained my excuse-note scam. They were delighted.

"What a brilliant way to cut school!" they agreed.

I bet a couple of them also had a girlfriend with impeccable handwriting.

HOW I GOT REVENGE ON A SCHOOL BULLY

There was a bully in high school who also happened to be one of the biggest football players on the varsity team. He outweighed me by more than 100 pounds and took full advantage of the overmatch during a physical education class.

For reasons I don't recall, our teacher had us play full-contact football without helmets or body protection of any kind. This provided the bully an opportunity to line up nose-to-nose against me. As the quarterback of my squad called out his signals, I grew more anxious. I knew what was coming.

When the ball was finally hiked, Mr. Football threw up his thick arms and hit me hard on my forehead. As I was blown backwards, I saw stars in my eyes and then everything went black. He'd knocked me out cold. It took several minutes for me to regain my senses.

Another time, he inflicted his own brand of humiliation by ordering a few of his friends to hold me still while he kicked me in the ass several times. I was furious and swore he would pay for his disrespect and cowardice.

An opportunity for revenge happened one night as I approached a home where a party was underway. Parked at the curb was an old classic car that had been restored with great care and, I assume, at great expense. Everybody in school knew who owned the beauty—the bully, Mr. Football.

I couldn't hurt him physically. And he was too thick-headed to care about any verbal lashing I might attempt. He'd simply retaliate with fists or spit. What would a warrior do?

He'd discover his enemy's weakness, exploit it, and win the battle.

As the others joined the party, I pulled a knife out of my pocket and flattened all four of his shiny new tires. I also cut up the pristine new upholstery in the car's interior. But I wasn't done.

The point of my knife was quite sharp. It was the perfect font for scratching up his glistening new paint job. I could have gone at it with a frenzy of angry, vengeful slashes, circles and jagged lines. Instead, at the rear fender I pushed my blade point into the enamel and moved toward the front of the car, making one long rude horizontal scratch line. I did the same on the other side of the car. It sent a message: Hey, boss, your perfect car isn't perfect anymore.

I never had a chance to ask the bully if he believed in karma.

THE LOWDOWN ON
HIGH STAKES LIVING

"My dad was a gambler and I'm one too."

—Aly Bruner

LIFE WITHOUT RISK IS A LIFE NOT WORTH LIVING

There was a time in my life, about 1983, when I was on the wild side, in the fast lane and doing drugs. During part of this time I was dating a gal named Rita, who had no barriers and was game for just about anything. We made a road trip to Calistoga in Northern California looking for adventure and we found it.

High on cocaine, looking for something fun to do, we decided to rent a pilot and glider plane. After being towed to a high altitude, the pilot was giving us a scenic tour that was beautiful but boring. I asked the young pilot if the glider was capable of aerobatics. The young pilot responded with a big grin. "Of course." My immediate response was, "Go for it, let's see what this baby can do."

Instantly he started doing maneuvers that were better than a roller coaster or anything you might find at an amusement park. He was doing loops with incredible G force, flying upside down, forcing stalls and doing spins. The ride was supposed to last for half an hour, but he was having so much fun we went overtime.

Finally, it was time to settle down and land. To my surprise a big crowd had gathered to watch our spectacle in the sky. I turned to the pilot and said, "That was awesome. Let's do it again."

After paying for another trip, once again we were pulled into the higher realms and I repeated, "Let it all hang out and don't hold back."

To my disappointment, the pilot explained that his boss saw what we were doing on the previous flight and chewed his ass out.

"Sorry, Aly, but he told me if I ever did that kind of thing again he would fire me."

Boy, was I disappointed. The ride was incredibly boring, and I was pissed off. When we landed, Rita and I jumped into my Ferrari 308 GTB and popped the clutch. My rear tires spun so fast and hard they tore up the grass.

Soon we were back on a descending, winding two-lane highway that I knew well, having made the trip over 100 times. Higher than a kite I decided it was time to show my date what the car could really do.

"Are you up for some excitement?" I knew what her answer would be.

I stomped the petal to the metal, driving like a bat out of hell. In the past, I'd never seen Highway Patrol or Sheriff's Department vehicles on this road, but this time—ooops— we flew by a lawman sitting in his car, having lunch. We were traveling well over 130 miles per hour.

I heard his siren first and then saw his flashing lights as he chased us down the hilly country highway. I knew he didn't have our license plate number because we flew by him too fast. So I cast a mischievous look at Rita and offered a big grin that basically said, I'm going to go for it.

I downshifted immediately and floored the gas pedal. No worries. By then I had a long history of racing in the United States. I held track records and had a California state championship under my belt. This is going to be a piece of cake, I thought.

There was not that much traffic ahead and I had no problem weaving in and out without having to back off the throttle. In the straightaway we reached speeds of 160 miles per hour. My adrenaline was peaking but I felt comfortable that there was no way in the world that the highway cop could catch me.

It wasn't long before we ran into some traffic, so I swerved out into the opposite lane on a straightaway and passed eight cars in one hellaciously fast sweep. The cop was nowhere in sight and I knew we had a huge lead because after the straightaway the road got very twisty again, which would slow him down. On the other hand, common sense told me that the cop would have radioed ahead to set up a roadblock. What to do?

It was late in the evening just before dark and I felt the best way out of the situation was to ditch the car out of sight and wait it out. After explaining the plan to my companion, we looked for a good place to hide. It was a delicious thought because we were in wine country, and the fields were covered with grape vines.

Finally, up ahead, we noticed a large group of tall trees and behind them an old barn. I slammed on the brakes, turned right, and slowed down so that my tires would not raise dust on the dirt road.

The spot was perfect for a fun-loving couple on the run. There was no way we would be spotted from the road. Yet we could hear the siren closing the distance and held our breath as we waited the several minutes it took him to speed by our turn-off. What a relief!

Assuming we'd be wise to hang out for a couple hours, we made ourselves comfortable by sprawling on a blanket we pulled from the car with a picnic basket full of food and a bottle of wine. I popped the cork and filled our glasses.

Then it dawned on me that we still had some cocaine, and there was no reason to let it go to waste. Also, we dared not have any in possession in case, by chance, Mr. Highway Patrolman found us. Rita and I quickly snorted the white powder and were feeling good—for about fifteen minutes.

As night fell and embraced us in darkness, I filled our glasses and made a robust toast, sharing a heart-felt philosophy.

"Life without risk is a life not worth living," I said.

One sip later I could not believe my eyes as a caravan of eight patrol cars, with both California Sheriff and Highway Patrol insignias, turned off the highway onto our intimate country road. They were right on top of us and I was baffled. How could they know our hiding spot?

Before any cops got out of their cars, I turned to Rita and gave her our game plan.

"Admit to nothing. We're just here having a picnic. Say nothing else. They never got an ID as to who was driving or a license plate number."

The beams of multiple flashlights blinded us. Without getting up, I raised my glass with a cocky attitude and offered, "Glass of wine anybody?" Only stern looks followed so I asked, "What seems to be the problem?"

The leader of the pack, a sergeant with a big pot belly spouted out, "You're under arrest."

"Really? Who are you arresting and why?"

Then I stood up to reveal the overmatch they'd walked into. I am a 6-foot-5-inch man. I looked down at the blustering sergeant whose eyes came to about the middle button on my shirt. He began to yell.

"We know it was you!"

I stayed calm. "What are you talking about? Are we under arrest for trespassing? We're just having a picnic."

The sergeant began to stutter with rage. "We've been after your ass for reckless driving, avoiding arrest, speeding over 120 miles per hour, and, and, and, we've got your ass!"

"Wasn't me, man." Then I went down my mental list of details. What kind of car were you chasing? Who was driving, man or a woman? "As you can see, we've just been sitting here having a nice picnic and some wine."

My attitude pissed him off even more. It was obvious that no one could make a proper identification as to what the driver looked like or who had been steering my Ferrari.

He began to belly bump me— again and again and again— yelling, "We know it was you!" I had to believe that he kept belly bumping me in an attempt to anger me. If I took a swing at him, they could arrest me. I let him go on a bit longer, then said, "Are you aware that I have seven witnesses here who can testify that you are assaulting me?"

That backed him off for a moment, and then he repeated his claim, "We know It was you. No woman could ever drive like that!"

I couldn't believe my ears. Then Rita, the lone female in the crowd, who was high on cocaine and angry, shot back, "Oh yeah? It *was* me driving." Now my ears were stinging. What a stupid mistake. An unforced error.

I wanted to pull her aside and explain that they couldn't prove anything on us including who was driving or if it was my car.

They wasted no time putting Rita in handcuffs while the pot-bellied sergeant taunted my manhood. "Are you going to let her take this beef?"

No reply.

I watched as they loaded my girlfriend into a patrol car. Then they took away my Ferrari keys.

"What are you doing?" I protested. "You can't take my keys, you have no right."

"You've had too much to drink." The sergeant gloated.

"You've got to be kidding. I'm sober as can be. Give me a sobriety test."

He ignored me as I continued to demand a test. When he wouldn't respond, I said, "Watch this," and began walking on my hands around the Ferrari. "Could I do that if I was intoxicated?"

The vehicle carrying Rita rolled past me. The look on her face was not her usual wild-girl grin. The other cars followed in a dusty parade.

"Come on. Jump in. I'll drive you in."

The lone Highway Patrolman who remained waved me to his car. "I'll take you to the jail where she will be booked."

I always traveled with cash, so I had several thousand dollars in my pocket. I waited a fairly long time before I was allowed to bail her out. Then they gave back my keys and then drove Bonnie and Clyde out to the barn and tree grove so that the dastardly criminals could retrieve their getaway car.

On the road home I chewed out Rita. "What the hell were you thinking? They had nothing on us, and they couldn't even identify the driver."

She was glum. She'd been booked for reckless driving, evading arrest, and more than I can remember.

The next day I called my attorney and told him the whole story. I also explained that we had a lot of leverage to clear Rita. There were seven witnesses that saw the sergeant assault me.

"It was only belly bumping, but nevertheless that's assault, and I want to file a complaint to press charges," I said.

A few days later I was contacted by Internal Affairs to investigate the complaint I'd filed. They had already verified my story by interviewing the other cops.

Soon after, IA representatives came to my house for a personal visit. They were giving me the opportunity—putting the squeeze on me, actually—in an attempt to save the sergeant's ass.

"I know what you're trying to do. You want me to drop the charges." Then I offered a solution. "This is really easy, guys. Drop the charges on Rita and give us a written apology from the sergeant."

They said the best they could do would be to reduce the charge to a simple speeding ticket, even though they knew I had been the driver.

"Fine," I said. "Tell the sergeant I'll drop the charges as soon as I receive his letter of apology for assaulting me."

When it was all resolved, I was still unsatisfied. There was a riddle that needed to be solved. The internal affairs officer was at my house and asked how they had found Rita and me behind the barn and under the trees.

"Did you notice the house behind the barn? A Fish and Game officer lives there. He had been listening to the chase on his radio scanner when he saw your Ferrari drive down the road and stop behind his barn. Naturally, he called the Highway Patrol."

I chuckled. Life without risk is a life not worth living.

SET UP TO BE BUSTED FOR DRUGS

The phone call should have made me happy. After all, I recognized the voice. It was Tony, an acquaintance I'd played poker with, and he said he had the $600 owed me from a gambling debt. Good deal. Or so I thought.

The knock on the door was not Tony with cash. It was the police and they arrived with a search warrant.

"What are you looking for?" I asked.

I soon learned that I was suspected of using my diamond business as a cover to deal drugs. This was an untrue and outrageous accusation. And it came at a very inopportune time: I was sitting at the kitchen table in my home with a very good client who was interested in buying diamonds.

I watched helplessly as the police ransacked my beautiful home and found nothing. They demanded that I open a safe I had in the house to lock up expensive merchandise, but all they found was a collection of high-grade diamonds and $25,000 in cash. No drugs.

The lead officer was blunt. "We'll get you next time, for sure."

Next time? Why would there be a next time? I didn't deal drugs.

A few days later I called Tony and asked him to drop by the house so that we could have a talk. I had to find out why the cops showed up after he called about a debt. We sat in my car because I feared the house might be bugged or under police surveillance.

"Tony, what's going on?"

It took a while, but finally he spilled the beans.

"Look, Aly, I know you don't deal drugs. But I was busted for a burglary and I had to give the cops something to make a deal."

"You told them I'm a drug dealer?"

"It was a plea bargain."

"Yeah, and the raid lost me a good client who doesn't want to be associated with a crooked dealer, and it could ruin my business if word gets around."

"You're missing the point."

"You told the cops that I—"

"But I knew you don't deal drugs, Aly. I knew they'd find nothing, and life would go on. It got me out of a jam."

I told him my home had been tossed and the whole scene had been very troubling for me. Then I said, "And what about the six hundred bucks?" I don't think he ever paid it back.

Tony didn't realize that I'd recorded the conversation so that I could take it to the police. I wanted them to hear Tony admit that he was lying from the get-go.

Alston, my father, accompanied me and after police listened to the tape recording, he insisted that they give me a lie detector test. Fortunately, at that time in my life, I had never even seen cocaine, except in movies. I was clean. Nothing to hide.

After the polygraph, the examiner told police that I was the most honest person he'd ever tested.

I was relieved when police officials gave me a written letter of apology. But that didn't win back the client who was in my home when the cops arrived. The damage had been done. He would never do business with me again.

Lesson learned: Be careful about the company you keep.

CHP ALMOST CAUGHT US BUT WE GOT AWAY

I am guilty of getting away with a lot of things while I was using cocaine. A girl who was one of my druggie friends wanted to do some cocaine, so we drove up Pala Verdes Road next to Interstate 580. I had a four-wheel-drive Chevy Blazer, so I put it in low gear and crawled up a very steep slope to a plateau where we could park and overlook the highway. At that height I believed there was no way we could get caught doing coke. Boy, was I wrong.

As we got the party started snorting cocaine in my SUV, I didn't have a care in the world. Then I heard tap, tap, tap on my driver's side window. I turned and discovered a California Highway Patrol officer. He must have walked up the hill. Maybe he'd seen my vehicle climbing to the ridge. In any case, I knew I was in deep shit if I got caught with cocaine.

In a frenzy, I put my Chevy in gear and took off, speeding in the opposite direction of the highway traffic, a good 100 yards below us. The bank was very steep, but if I was going to escape, I had only one option. I figured, what the heck, my four-wheel-drive was all-terrain. I'd just creep down the steep bank slowly.

Wrong again because the grass on the slope was wet, so my tires began to slip, and before I knew it the Blazer was fishtailing. It felt like we were water skiing, and on another occasion, I might have whooped it up and had some fun. Not this time. When the Blazer tilted and began to roll down the hill sideways, and I realized we had not buckled our seatbelts, my drugged friend and I were tossed around like stuffed toys.

Our bodies banged against the ceiling, then we were thrown back down into our seats, and for a time it seemed the rock 'n' roll roller coaster ride would never end.

Miraculously, after several rotations, cascading down the steep bank sideways, we landed upright on Interstate 580—but all four tires were flat. So what! We had to make a getaway, so I very slowly headed west toward Castro Valley.

As we made our great escape, on the other side of the highway a CHP vehicle appeared with lights flashing and sirens screaming. The driver slowed to a crawl and gave us a good, long look before picking up speed. I assumed it was headed toward the turnoff where it could meet up with the officer who had trudged up the slope and kindly tapped on my window.

I guess you might say I had escaped twice.

Somehow even with flat tires moving at a crawl we disappeared into the night, relieved and still high from the adrenalin.

THREE RUN-INS WITH FISH & GAME

I had several run-ins in my life with fish and game. One of the most memorable was when we went fishing underneath Fanny Bridge in Tahoe City, California.

The historic bridge earned its name because girls would often bend over the railing to look at the giant rainbow trout that gathered in the green-blue water below, thereby exposing their "fannies" to motorists driving through the narrow passage. Since the bridge's reputation is a little bit naughty, I blame it for inspiring a fishing expedition with my friend Eddie.

The waterway enjoyed a bevy of gorgeous trout because it was the only outlet from Lake Tahoe. It was a fisherman's dream, which is probably why the California Department of Fish and Wildlife made it illegal to cast a hook and line into the water.

Eddie and I hid under the bridge until three o'clock in the morning. We figured it was too late for pedestrians to stroll on the bridge, and early enough to get our work done before dawn. We caught so many giant rainbow trout that they filled an ice chest to the brim.

As the sun rose, it was time for breakfast, so Eddie and I went to a local restaurant. As we entered, we had no choice but to sit next to the two fish and game officers who were enjoying a meal at the counter. Eddie was kind of a smart ass. I should have known he'd push the envelope by engaging the officers in conversation.

"Hey, has anybody ever tried fishing underneath Fanny bridge?"

My body tensed. I thought he was pretty crazy to bring that up because we had an ice chest full of illegal rainbow trout in the bed of our truck—and some of their fins were sticking up in the air it was so full. The officers replied with the certainty of authority.

"Oh yeah. Some have tried but we've caught them all."

"Did they do jail time, or just pay a fine?" Eddie grinned as he baited the officers. I tried to smile but all I wanted was to get the heck out of there—before they checked out our truck full of illegal rainbow trout.

I was very angry at Eddie. I couldn't believe he was foolish enough to talk to the fish and game officers. After we left the diner, I gave him a real ass chewing.

"They might've thrown us in jail because of your big mouth!"

He shrugged. That was Eddie.

But I must admit, those trout definitely tasted better after the scare I endured at the diner. When we shared our catch with a few friends, we told them the whole story about what happened at Fanny Bridge and breakfast. They all laughed and said, "Bruner, only you and Eddie could've pulled that off."

* * *

In 1977 my friend Frank and I set out to go hunting. The only problem was we chose Point Reyes National Seashore, a natural sanctuary overseen by the U.S. National Parks

Service. We liked that location because I saw myself as a big game hunter and I was always hungry for record-setting feats. Bragging rights. Trophies. In this case, the monster fallow deer in a haven where no hunting was allowed. Call me crazy, or maybe just call me drunk on risk. I loved risk. I drank it for breakfast. For me, it was a natural high. Without risk, what was life?

As the mastermind of the expedition, I had Frank drop me off after we did a few days of scouting driving the roads, looking out for fish and game officers and I had finally spotted a monster fallow deer that had the potential of being a possible world record. The fallow deer is a common species native to Europe. But it has been introduced to various nations. That kind of prize is every deer hunter's dream.

I shot a magnificent fallow deer just before nightfall with the hope that I could return in the dead of night to haul it out. To my surprise, fish and game   officers were nearby and heard the shot. I knew the hunt was on to find me because at first I heard a Jeep coming and then I heard the voices of officers, about thirty yards away.

"He's got to be here somewhere," said one officer.

Darn right. I was too close for my comfort. So I hid in the bushes, covered my rifle with brush and waited until I was sure they had left the area. Then I began hiking up a trail to put some distance between me and the felled deer.

Frank, meanwhile, couldn't understand why I wasn't at the pickup spot we'd chosen. I kept delaying my arrival because I didn't dare emerge until after it was pitch black. Finally, after a long wait, I saw his headlights approaching the area where we had agreed to meet and I started running helter-skelter down the hill. My speed and momentum were picking up pretty good when I slammed against the sanctuary's barbed wire barrier, which was invisible in the dark. My stomach and arms were cut up badly. Even worse, my body was snagged by the sharp barbs and hung against the fence for quite a while before I could get loose. In pain, I limped to Frank's car and after gingerly folding myself into the passenger seat, I told him to get us the heck out of there.

Despite my wounds, I had Frank drop me off the next day so I could retrieve my rifle and dress my game. I skinned out the hide, cutting the head off so that I could do shoulder mount at a taxidermist. I registered it in the Records of Exotics, Volume 2, 1978, edition as a new world record because of the size of the antlers.

* * *

Trespassing the National Historic Landmark Hearst Castle in the late 1970s was another example of my dangerous stunts. This time, my friend Tim and I were in search of African Aoudad, a species of sheep that roamed on the site's thousands of acres.

We sped up a mountain slope on all-terrain motorcycles after cutting through a barbed wire fence. Once we reached Little Pico Creek, we left the motorcycles nearby so the sheep wouldn't hear us coming. All day we hunted with no results. So we returned to our motorcycles and discovered that somebody, probably castle constables, had thrown them into a deep hole in the creek. After all, we knew the grounds were patrolled by aircraft. Whenever we heard a plane coming, we hid underneath trees or bushes. Needless to say, we had been discovered and had to dive into the deep hole with our clothes on to retrieve our motorcycles from the creek.

We were soaking wet by the time we returned to my truck. So we loaded the bikes up and headed to a nearby town to find a laundromat to dry our clothes. We stripped to our shorts and shoved them in a dryer. The lady who operated the laundromat brought us towels. "You can take off your shorts and dry them too."

Kindness? In truth, the gesture made us nervous. The wet clothing was a clue, a tell-all sign. The clothes could tie us to the creek.

It was such a close call that we never again attempted to hunt at Hearst Castle.

SNOWMOBILE ACCIDENT

When Taryn was twelve years old, we went snowmobiling up the West Fork of Morgan Creek in Idaho. She rode double on a Polaris snowmobile with her friend Kelly. It was a gorgeous day. The snow at the bottom was about two feet deep, and when we got to the top of the ridge, the snow was more than three feet deep.

This spot was very popular, so the road up the mountain was nicely packed down from other snowmobiles. That made our climb fairly easy.

On top, the beautiful snow made me a little giddy. I took off in my own direction and suddenly realized I was flying in mid-air, shooting off a 150-foot cliff. My snowmobile crashed into a tree, but by then my body was already sailing elsewhere. When I landed the snow was so deep it felt like a featherbed, so my body didn't suffer. But there were still a couple big problems: I'd just had knee surgery, so I knew it was going to be difficult and painful to walk down the mountain. More importantly, I wasn't sure Taryn and Kelly saw what had happened. Then I heard her calling for me. "Dad!" But she couldn't hear me respond.

After the girls searched for me with no luck, Taryn, fearing the worse, drove her Polaris snowmobile for five miles to where we had parked my Suburban SUV. For safety reasons, in case of emergency, I always left a set of keys on top of the left front tire.

Attached to the vehicle was the trailer I used to haul the snowmobiles. Somehow Taryn figured out how to detach the trailer and then began the ten-mile drive home—despite having absolutely no driving experience.

When she arrived, she ran into our house screaming and crying.

"I think Dad's dead!"

Nancy, alarmed but calm, asked what had happened.

"He drove off a cliff and crashed into a tree!"

Nancy was still confused. How had the girls made it home? There was not enough snow on the roads for a snowmobile.

"I drove the Suburban after disconnecting the trailer," Taryn said.

Nancy loaded up the car with Remington, our French Briard sheep dog, and returned to the West Fork Morgan Creek Road to try and find me. She searched in the deep snow for about thirty minutes with no luck. Then she and the girls went to get help and called an emergency number to alert a search and rescue squad. Taryn led the way, guiding the professionals to where she thought I may have fallen off the cliff.

By that point, I was already walking down the mountain. They found me on the road.

I was sorry I'd given the girls such a scare. But I was very proud of Taryn. Looking back, I'm still amazed that she navigated a potential disaster while learning how to drive.

TREASURE HUNTING IN MANTA BAY ECUADOR

Many people dream of discovering treasure that will make them rich. It is exciting to hunt for huge rewards and even when I was doing well selling diamonds, I yearned for more risk and a sense of adventure.

That's probably why I was all ears when Kevin Wong and Margaret Brandeis visited my office and told me a tale about a sunken ship off the coast of Ecuador. They'd learned about me after reading one of the newspaper articles written about my exploits and correctly assumed I be might interested in a deep-sea treasure hunt for a Spanish Galleon named the Santa Maria de Los Remedios that was built in 1587 and sank the following year after being battered in a powerful storm.

They told me how they'd become intrigued after meeting Robert Marx, an American man who'd become a pioneer in scuba diving and an expert in finding sunken treasure. The manifest for the Santa Maria de los Remedios promised a lot of treasure— 174 tons of silver and 11.9 tons of gold— and Marx knew where the ship likely lay at the bottom of the ocean. He was a reliable source because he'd had found over 5,000 ships that had been lost at sea.

We bought the information from Marx, who was entitled to 10 percent of whatever we found. In the end, Kevin, Margaret and I spent $3 million to find it. The cost included paying bribes to several government officials to get permission to search for treasure in Manta Bay Ecuador. We also had to agree to give Ecuador 50 percent of our discovery.

As one of the major investors, I could scuba dive with the team hired to find the treasure. My job was to use a metal detector in the general area with the hope of locating cannons, which would lead us to the ship. The ocean dives also allowed me to spear fish to provide food for the crew. Margaret also made cake from lard which tasted horrible. I also slept on the ship in a bunk bed. We were roughing it at sea.

I also went ashore to the city of Montecristi, where artisans made Panama hats that were woven so tightly you could roll them up and shove them through a jewelry ring.

Another adventure was traveling to the jungle to meet the indigenous people and buy their crafts, which I considered treasures in themselves.

Our contract with the Ecuador stated that we were expected to divide anything we found every 10 days. In the beginning, we found a lot of broken pottery. But when the government's representative met with us to divide our findings, he reneged on the agreement and wouldn't even let us anything. We could see the writing on the wall. If they coveted broken pottery, what would they do when we began pulling gold and silver from the shipwreck?

We had no choice but to throw in the towel, pack our bags and go home. It's one thing to lose your own money because you enjoy the thrill of it all. But let me tell you, it is no fun telling others that we had lost our entire investment, as well as years of planning and time on the high seas. This was particularly painful because I'd convinced several friends to put some money into the adventure.

Yet if you wager nothing you win nothing. Every true treasure hunter knows this. And nobody goes through a life of risk without absorbing some losses.

FINDING PARADISE

———————————————

"Nancy, do you think we should close the center?"
"How do you put a price on saving people's lives?"

—Aly & Nancy

NANCY, THE LOVE OF MY LIFE

It was a very unusual way that I met Nancy. I was going through a horrible divorce with Donna, who would eventually be my ex-wife. Nancy was the designated driver for a group of gals who were enjoying a fun night out, and that's how it happened that Donna introduced me to her in 1990 at a Blackhawk Country Club party in Danville, California.

I concluded that Nancy was the woman I wanted to connect with for the rest of my life while we chatted at a table and I sipped a few glasses of wine. She was the most fascinating woman I had ever met, and she had a twinkle in her eye and a smile that made me melt.

At one point, I excused myself to go to the restroom. Standing at the urinal, I listened as a guy who'd been dancing with Donna sang her praises and suggested that a toss in the hay was likely after the party.

"Did you see that gal I was dancing with? Boy, am I going to have fun with her tonight."

I laughed. "She's my wife and she's really not that good."

When I returned to the party looking for Nancy, I found her sitting on the lap of a friend who was perched on a barstool. I had to figure out a way how to lure her off that man's lap, so I got down on my hands and knees, took off her shoe, and began sucking her toes. It was convenient that she wasn't wearing stockings. My mouth on her flesh made her laugh profusely. Not only did I get her off his lap, but she agreed to sit down at a table again to talk. There was no need for another glass of wine. We were only interested in learning more about each other.

"I'd like to see you again," I confessed.

We talked a bit more before she gave me her phone number and agreed to allow me to call her. Two days later I asked her out on a date.

"I'll have to get back to you, Aly."

I wasn't sure why she needed time but accepted her way of doing things.

Later I would learn that she wouldn't date me without first asking Donna's permission.

"Sure, go ahead. He's a lot of fun," Donna had told her.

At first glance, that might seem generous. Technically, Donna and I were still married, though our relationship had ended long before. As it turned out, Donna encouraged Nancy because she wanted her friend to be a spy. Nancy could date me if she was willing to figure out if I was hiding money somewhere—money that my dear wife could go after in our divorce proceedings. Nancy would have nothing to do with spying on me for Donna. In fact, she helped me during the divorce proceedings which lasted for years.

After that first date, I couldn't let a day go by without calling her. On our first date we went out to dinner and ended up going to my house, bringing home a nice bottle of wine. We talked until the wee hours. I was learning more about her that convinced me even more that someday after the divorce this was the woman I would want to marry.

After several dates I learned that we had some huge contrasts to consider. Nancy had graduated from Stanford

University and earned a lifetime teaching credential, whereas I didn't even have a high school diploma. She had taught high school for ten years, including United States history, a topic I'd flunked in high school, and she also taught French. The latter gave me an idea.

"Have you ever been to Paris?"

"No."

I found it unusual that a French teacher had never been to France. On the spot I made a secret commitment to take her to Paris sometime in the future. *Our* future.

I also learned that Nancy was divorced but did not have children. Donna and I had two girls, Taryn and Tawny. I also had a son and daughter, Matthew and Jessica, from a previous marriage. As our relationship grew, Nancy generously went with me to all my son's baseball games and enjoyed several outings I'd arranged with my kids. Through the years she has loved my children as though they were her own.

Nancy and I soon became inseparable and after three months we decided to live together. There were many reasons our relationship continued to thrive, but I'll always be grateful that she stayed with me despite my divorce battle with Donna, which stretched on for years, turned ugly, and threatened my financial stability.

We remained a live-in couple for almost ten years. That was by design. I figured that within that time frame, she would learn all the good sides and bad sides about me and I would learn the same about her. I'd also told her that when it was time to marry, I would not demand a prenuptial agreement.

"I want the marriage to last, Nancy. That's all that matters to me."

Even the wedding was unique. We invited friends to a New Year's Eve party without telling them that we intended to exchange wedding vows that night. When my daughter Taryn learned what we intended to do, she turned to Nancy and said, "Promise me you'll never get a divorce." If divorce had been tough on me, it had also left its mark on my children. Plus, all my kids loved Nancy.

We timed it so that we were married one second after midnight, so that we could claim we were the first couple married in the year 2000. One of my friends who didn't come to the New Year's Eve party said, "If I would've known you were getting married I would've been there." My comment back was, "If you're not a good enough friend to come to our New Year's Eve party you're not a good enough friend to come to our wedding."

MAKING PAYROLL

I had some obligations to take care of and business was slow which led me to take a risk I normally would not take. Unless, of course, I was flush.

I was not flush.

It was Friday and on Monday I had to make payroll and accounts payable totaling $54,000. I had never missed payroll; I'd always paid my bills on time. I take that stuff seriously and as a result I'd earned the respect of a lot of notable notables. Nancy Reagan, for instance, was pleased with the $300,000 I'd helped raised for her drug awareness program. And there were many others who respected my business success and the responsible way I ran my operation.

But here I was with an ugly shortfall.

My girlfriend Nancy Del Colletti has all the numbers in her head—and a lot more. I rely on her to keep things straight. I turned to her and asked, "How much do we have in the bank?"

She shot me a nervous look and delivered the grim news. "We have fifteen thousand … and some change."

"Fifteen grand. Okay. Here's what we're going to do. Buy round-trip tickets to Las Vegas with a credit card and go get our money—in cash. All of it."

Oh, she loved that. Here we go again. She rolled her beautiful eyes and sighed because she knew exactly what I was up to.

On Saturday we drove to the airport, landed in Sin City without incident ,and then checked into the Rio All-Suite

Hotel & Casino. We were given a suite because I was a known commodity: I had gambled there often and was a high roller in the casino rating system. All the Vegas casinos can access this rating system so they know who is tossing the dice and whether or not the gambler in question pays his markers promptly. I've already told you: I pay to play. No problem there.

In the past, the casinos always gave me a $30,000/$50,000 line of credit, and all the food and drink from room service and restaurants were complimentary. Nice. In earlier years when business was going like gangbusters I was considered a *player*. I used to risk backgammon for $1,000 a point with other big boys, winning as much as $40,000 in an afternoon. And at the casinos I always bought in for $5,000 and played with $500 poker chips.

We didn't dawdle. Soon after checking into our room, I put on my game face. It was ShowTime.

We strolled out of the elevator and headed for the action with cash in hand. I hit the craps table buying in at my normal five large. I gave Nancy a thousand bucks.

"*Go for it.* I'll stay here while you hit the blackjack table."

"No way."

"Why?" I was a bit perturbed. I had a plan and a $54K debt to pay on Monday.

"I'm uncomfortable making big bets. You can find me at The Derby," she said.

Oh, God, I thought, a horse race game at the quarter machines. You could bet as many silver pieces as you wanted on each horse. Just like the racetrack. It was fun and almost as exciting as going to the Kentucky Derby because the odds changed on every race and the casino's mechanical horses raced on an oval track, around which about fifteen gamblers would sit, cheering their fillies. But could you make a killing at that venue? I had my doubts.

But as I watched her disappear into the crowd, I knew Nancy had her own way of doing things. While most of the other people would play the favorites, she favored playing the long shots. Hey, we were in Las Vegas to win and win big. Go with your gut.

Meanwhile, I hit the craps table hard. For a while, I was on a roll, tossing the dice for fifteen to twenty minutes straight, betting a thousand dollars on each round. My $5,000 grew to $28,300, but all good things must come to an end. I crapped out losing $8,000. It was time to find other kinds of fun. I gave the casino employee who was placing my bets a $300 tip, and with $20,000 to play with went looking for Nancy. That's when I heard screams, hooting, and hollering on the other side of the casino.

By the time I arrived a crowd had gathered around a machine. I moved closer and realized Nancy was the center of attention. Lo and behold, my better half was raking in the dough. Big bucks. It was overwhelming and exhilarating. Yet alarming, too, because she was dumping money on the extra-long shots 20/80 to 1. I had to sit.

"What the heck are you doing? You hardly ever win on the long shots."

She laughed.

"*Loser?* I've been playing the long-shots since I got here."

As it turned out, while I was crapping out, her timing with the ponies could not have been better. After a couple bets, she explained, the bells and whistles went off and quarters quickly filled her bucket. Her cup had runneth over so violently, one race after another, that a cashier ran to her rescue, turning off the victory lights and sirens several times before explaining that she'd have to go to the cashier's window to be paid her entire winnings: There were not enough quarters in the machines.

And the ritual didn't stop after a couple lucky bets; it went on and on. Nancy was killing it with so many long shots that the growing crowd of tourists and players were baffled and in a frenzy to know her secret. After all, many of them had been dropping quarters for hours yet had not seen their long shots take the cake. I have never seen her have so much fun.

Stanford might want to consider giving Nancy some sort of honorary degree. Not that she didn't already have the kind you get the old-fashioned way—by earning it.

I was hungry so Nancy called it quits and we cashed in her buckets of quarters. In return, she received a huge stack of hundred dollar bills. We took a moment to count our winnings plus the $15,000 we started with. It totaled $39,500. Holy Moley. We were well over the halfway mark of meeting our debt.

On our way to lunch we passed the sports betting section of the casino.

"Nancy, you're a diehard 49ers fan. Who are they playing this weekend?"

"Atlanta."

We stared up at the electronic board where the odds were displayed.

"Cool," I said. "The Niners are a six-point underdog."

I immediately turned to place a bet, but Nancy grabbed my arm and stopped me.

"Aly, are you crazy? No way. San Francisco usually loses in Atlanta."

"Nancy, you got to know when to hold 'em and know when to fold 'em. Like that Kenny Rogers song, remember?" I tried to sing the chorus; it didn't sound so good. "Lady luck has been with us so far and I have a good feeling the Niners are going to win."

Nancy's answer was more a groan than spoken word. She was nearly hysterical with anxiety as I pushed $20,000 worth of $500 poker chips toward the cashier.

"Let it ride. We'll take the Niners plus-6," I said.

Nancy yanked me away from the window, waving a finger in my face. "No! Don't you dare!"

"Okay, okay. I won't bet it all."

But her protest continued. No matter how much I taunted her, in a friendly way, about her hero Joe Montana, she wouldn't back down. Finally, I'd had enough; we were making a scene.

"Go away, Nancy. Go to the restaurant and reserve us a table. I'll be right with you."

Behind her back I went ahead and laid down a bet for $20,000 of $500 chips, plus I took $7500 in cash that I had my pocket for a total bet of $27,500.

We were exhausted. And it didn't help when at dinner I showed her the voucher for the huge bet I'd just laid down. She was furious. Her silence was more unnerving than the tongue lashing a sane man might have expected.

In our suite, Nancy tossed and turned all night. The hefty bet, the fear of losing, would not let her sleep. I was calm as a cucumber feeling great about the bet.

The next morning Nancy was not talkative at breakfast and the tension was thick. I was in the proverbial doghouse and couldn't help ponder what would happen if I didn't have sufficient funds by Monday.

Finally, it was game time. We turned on the television to watch. After kick off, I don't know what was more entertaining: watching the game or watching Nancy panic. She could not sit but for a moment and was running back and forth between the bed and the sofa. Every play was life or death to her. And when the Niners fell behind Nancy almost had a coronary. She couldn't watch, and I was laughing so hard my stomach hurt.

"No big deal," I assured her, referring to the spread. "We have six points."

Who wouldn't place their money on Joe Montana? His reputation was that of a cool, calm operator who never let the pressure get to him. I recalled a story about him that is now well-known.

Joe, in a tight playoff game with mere seconds left on the clock, had driven his team to the 35-yard line. But San Francisco was down by six points and needed a touchdown to win. Yet in the huddle to call the next play, the first thing out of Joe's mouth was, "Boys, did you see that gorgeous blonde on the 50-yard line?" Then he named the play, and said, "Let's do it. Cover me, boys."

Now Joe was in the same situation. With much on the line—maybe even my girlfriend—Nancy and I glued our eyes to the TV as Joe took the snap and faded back. He was patient, waiting for a receiver to get open. For fans, true believers, and gamblers like me, it seemed like forever. Then suddenly Joe threw a strike, right on the numbers.

"Touchdown!" Nancy screamed. "We won! We won!"

I quickly tallied our treasury: The need win gave us a grand total of $64,500.

Then after subtracting expenses for the trip to the Entertainment Capital of the World, and paying payroll and accounts payable, I knew we still had a grub stake to play with.

Turning to Nancy, a shit-eating grin on my face. I said, "That leaves us with about eight grand. Fun money. Heck, shall we take the money and run or ... how about another roll of the dice?"

If she'd been wearing football cleats she would have kicked me—hard. Instead, she said, "It's time to go home."

HOW TO MAKE FRIENDS IN ITALY: REAR-END A BMW

I took Albert Butterfield and Steve Kane with my wife Nancy to Italy for a Formula One race. While we were there Nancy did some shopping to buy clothes. As we were wandering around Milan one evening we met Stefano and Barbara on the street and asked for advice for a good restaurant. They tried giving us directions to one of their favorite restaurants, but we couldn't understand them. They said they would show us so I asked them to join us for dinner and we became very close friends.

The next day Albert, Steve, Nancy, and I were headed out for dinner to meet up with Stefano and Barbara. While I was driving I had on dress shoes with leather souls and I had to slam on the brakes on the freeway. I ended up rear-ending a black BMW twice because my foot slipped off the brake pedal, ending up hitting the throttle pedal two times. In Italy if you have an accident you must pull off the autostrada and use the call box to get the police.

When they arrived, they were dressed like Gestapo with their knee-high boots and carried machine guns. They took all our passports. Nancy was petrified. I called Stefano after the police arrived and Stefano came to the rescue, showing the police something indicating that one of his relatives was the chief of police for all of Italy. The people in the BMW called an ambulance, indicating that they had whiplash. I explained to the police officers that they were not wearing seatbelts. They didn't even give me a ticket. We posed for pictures with the police which Albert included in a book he wrote about the trip. Stefano gave Nancy his uncle's business card.

The next day Albert, Steve, and I went to the Formula One race in Monza. Nancy on the other hand went sightseeing and got pulled over by four police officers on motorcycles because the front license plate was missing from the accident. They didn't speak English, so she reached in her purse to show them the accident report. What she pulled out first was the card of the chief of police and they were stunned. They gave her a police escort with motorcycles back to the hotel. This card is now the "get out of jail free card." Unfortunately, it was only good in Italy.

STABBING AT LAX

An event in the year 1991 changed my life forever. Even to this day, I can close my eyes and not only remember the details but also experience the physical and emotional toll it took.

I was forty-one at the time, and my life had been turned upside down by a prolonged, nasty divorce that consumed all my time and much of my money to defend myself. Although my diamond business had been very profitable for years, I was desperate for more cash flow to replenish my coffers. When I received a phone call from Sheridan, a woman I had once dated, I was open to the business transaction she said she could facilitate.

Sheridan told me that she was related to the singer, songwriter, and actor Lou Rawls by way of his marriage to her cousin. She claimed he was interested in buying an expensive piece of jewelry for his wife as at gift. I was very excited and asked her to set up an appointment as soon as possible. Before we hung up, she insisted that I select only my finest pieces of diamond jewelry for Rawls to consider.

I went through my inventory in the safe I had in my office and put together an incredible selection of gifts fit for a queen. I also arranged for some additional pieces that I took on consignment. The total retail value of the collection I would share was valued at about $3 million.

When Sheridan assured me that the appointment had been set up and she would pick me up and escort me to Rawls' house, I had my girlfriend Nancy book my flight from San Francisco to the Los Angeles International Airport—despite my misgivings. Since this happened during the Gulf War, I knew the rules for carry-on items had changed. Therefore, I would not be allowed to carry the pistol I wore for personal protection onto the airplane. Also, from Sheridan's very first call, I had a funny feeling in the pit of my stomach. I was anxious and felt like something was going to happen. Yet I needed the cash flow so badly I agreed to the meeting.

Back in those days, friends and family could greet arrivals at the gate. Sheridan was there smiling as I bounded off the plane. Our talk was cordial as I followed her to the parking structure. Even so, in the middle of the airport she kept on repeating, "Follow me," and I was puzzled that the car wasn't parked on the lower level for convenience. She led me up a staircase to a second level where I quickly noticed that the parking area was empty—no cars filled the spaces—and this made me nervous.

I ran into the middle of the structure and found myself surrounded by three people, one woman and two men.

"Just drop the case of diamonds," one man said.

With a glance, I noticed Sheridan had remained some distance away, in a corner, just watching what was happening. I soon learned that the woman was Sheridan's sister and one of the men was her brother. They pulled out knives to intimidate me.

I am six feet, five inches tall, and at the time I was in good physical condition. Not to mention, I was holding a briefcase that contained my life savings and it was not insured against loss or theft.

"No way," I said, refusing the order to let go of my case.

The sister came at me from the front, jabbing at me with her sharp blade. I batted away her thrusts, using my briefcase as a shield to defend myself. That worked against her initial attempts, then I felt her knife as it found its mark and penetrated me dead center in the chest.

I collapsed to my knees with blood gushing, and she continued to lunge at me, until I had no choice but to drop my briefcase and grab the blade with my bare right-hand. The pain felt like scalding heat as my flesh was cut to the bone. To slow her attack, I clamped my left hand around her wrist but felt a body press against my back.

Sheridan's brother caught me from behind, and over my right shoulder flashed a knife. Before he could slash my throat, I ducked my head and felt white heat again as the sharp edge cut the top of my head, as though I were being scalped.

My briefcase, damaged while defending myself, was grabbed by the third person, a small man who did not appear to have a knife. With diamonds in hand, he quickly headed toward the stairs. If he made it to the ground level, I was sure I'd never see my precious cargo again. As I watched Sheridan and her brother also flee, I knew I had only one thing going for me. The diamonds had been packed with solid gold pieces that added some weight. Maybe that would slow them down.

That knowledge didn't do me much good, though, as I continued to tangle with the sister.

"Let go!" she shouted.

Miraculously, my clamp on her wrist was still firm, though I feared more knife wounds were possible.

"No! You'll only stab me again!" I said, as I got to my feet, looked her in the eye, and then shoved her away as hard as I could. She turned and ran after the others.

Again, I collapsed to my knees, battered by the realization that not only had my life savings been stolen, I would have to pay for the expensive jewelry I'd taken on consignment. I had to stop the thieves. But blood was gushing out of my chest and hand, and the thick flow from the head wound began to sting my eyes. My wavy hair was also an aggravation: It was shoulder length and dripping blood onto my white shirt. It was then that I realized my attackers had somehow pulled off my suit jacket, and a pool of my blood had spread on the concrete and soaked the knees of my pants.

How I got the strength, I don't know. First, I pressed my slashed hand against my stabbed chest, hoping the pressure would stop both from bleeding. Then I chased after my assailants, rushing down two flights of stairs.

On the ground level of the parking structure, I saw the thieves walking across several traffic lanes on their way to another parking structure. Once I was onto their trail, I was conscious of playing cat and mouse with them so they would not realize I was coming after them.

The next parking lot was crowded with parked and moving cars and people everywhere. In the middle of it all, my four would-be killers made their way to what I assumed was their getaway car. The small man carrying the briefcase was lagging behind the others. I seized the moment by running toward him, screaming my head off.

"Drop my case or I'll kill you!"

I must have looked like a maniac, a man covered in blood, flapping his arms, shouting, a character in a horror movie. The small man heard my voice, turned, and then must have panicked. He dropped the case and ran like hell.

I hobbled to the briefcase and couldn't believe my good fortune. I now had my life back! That didn't mean I was safe. Surrounded by stunned people who only wanted to make their flight or get home, I began to yell again and point at the group of thieves.

"Help me! Please. I've been robbed. They stabbed at me. Take a good look! Look at them!"

The four of them ran out of sight as I fell to the ground. A woman came to help.

"Please call an ambulance and the police," I said, nearly out of breath.

Police arrived, put on surgical gloves, and then pressed against my wounds to help stop the bleeding. One officer standing over me turned to his partner and said, "He's not going to make it." What an asshole!

Before I knew it, I was in an ambulance, lights flashing and siren screaming. I knew a little something about speed. It felt like we were going 100 miles an hour or more. We quickly arrived at UCLA Medical Center.

In the emergency room, a beautiful young doctor ran to me. A toy pink panther clung to the rubber end of her stethoscope. I began to flirt while she worked to save my life. I was so excited to have my gems and gold back in my possession I did not have a clue as to how close I was to death. Maybe that was a problem I had to rethink: I'd always thought I was invincible.

A staffer asked for contact information. I was still conscious, so I gave Nancy's name and phone number.

"But don't tell her what happened, okay?"

Later, Nancy would tell me that the moment she heard the staffer's voice she knew in her heart what had happened.

In the emergency room, I was given six units of blood and then whisked to the Intensive Care Unit. That's where police arrived to take a report on the robbery and stabbing. When I asked them to take possession of my briefcase, they refused. Routine procedure wouldn't allow it.

"But there's a fortune of value in it. I can't protect it in my condition."

A few hours later I suffered another fright when I got a phone call from Sheridan asking if I was okay. Surreal. I immediately thought, "My God, they're trying to find out what room I'm in so they can kill me—the victim and witness to their crime." Simple truth: No witness, no arrest.

After explaining my predicament to the attending physician, I was moved to another floor and registered in a false name. *Mario Sanchez.* To this day, I still have the wristband.

I thought I was safe, but Sheridan called again, and the receptionist at the front desk connected her to my room, exposing my whereabouts. How stupid was that? I was beside myself and insisted on changing names again—I still have my *William Jackson* wristband— and rooms. Then I told the hospital that only Nancy, alone, could visit or contact me.

From my new room, I called a friend in the diamond business, an importer in Los Angeles, and asked if he would come pick up my briefcase and lock it in his safe. He came immediately, and I began to breathe easier.

Against doctor's orders, I wanted to get out of the hospital ASAP. By then I'd been hospitalized for about three days, and they expected me to stay at least another week. I couldn't. The fear of another murder attempt haunted me. No doubt the pain medication had made my thinking unclear and stupid.

When Nancy flew to the City of Angels, she brought me fresh clothes and we decided to hop on a flight to San Francisco. I told my doctors that we had season tickets for the Golden State Warriors and an important game was coming up.

Like a Greek chorus, they said, no, no, no. Even a short flight would put me at risk. But to attend a basketball game, jostled by a huge, excitable crowd of sports fanatics? Stupid, stupid, stupid. They reminded me that I'd undergone an angiogram and the medical imaging method required that I be injected with a radio-opaque contrast so that doctors could visualize the insides of my blood vessels and organs— such as the heart chambers. This was serious stuff, they said.

Yet I rejected their advice, flew to the Golden City, and rooted for a National Basketball Team that would go 55-27 for the season, only to lose in the first round to the Seattle SuperSonics. What was I thinking? Or *not* thinking?

I yelled and cheered at the game with such vigor, I developed two hematomas in my groin, each the size of golf balls, and I had to be rushed to a local emergency room. The doctor asked, "What were you doing at the game? Why aren't you in a hospital?"

"I've got season tickets. I didn't want them to go to waste! But, Doc, I wasn't playing in the game. I was only watching it." My sense of humor had survived the attack.

The doctor insisted that I stay in bed for several days, and this time I agreed. The next day I learned that my escapade had made the news.

The San Francisco Chronicle Sporting Green section did a story on me. The headline read:

Warriors Fan Unfazed by Brush with Death

The article included details of my ambush, the stabbings, and my insistence that I attend the Warriors game. If only the same reporter had stayed in touch with me so that he could have reported the aftermath: Nancy's anger when Michael Jordon and the Chicago Bulls came to town. We couldn't attend because I was still recuperating.

It may have seemed like fun and games, until days after I'd returned home, I got another call from Sheridan. Police had already hooked up my phone so that I could record any phone conversations I might have.

The call was audacious. Sheridan tried to pretend that she too was a victim and did not have a clue as to who the assailants were. I believe she could tell by the way I talked on the phone that I was no dope and I was only trying to trap her into saying something incriminating.

Detective Bill Spiers from the Los Angeles Police Department flew upstate to show me mug shots so that I could identify the men and woman who assaulted me. Sheridan, her brother, and her sister were arrested, and we would go to trial. The third man, the small guy who had trouble hauling the diamonds and gold, was never arrested.

The drama didn't end there. I was tipped off by a mutual friend who had ties to the Hell's Angels motorcycle club: Sheridan and her accomplices had tried to hire the bikers to put out a contract out on me. The hope was that I'd be murdered before the trials. But the motorcycle club declined to get involved because I'd once sold jewelry to several members. Even so, my tipster warned me that she would not stop until she found someone else to do the job. I was shaken by the simple truth: No witness, no conviction.

After court dates had been set for the trial, I bought a bulletproof vest and thought about hiring a twenty-four-hour bodyguard, but never did.

Sheridan's brother was tried first and found guilty on all counts. When it came to the sentencing phase, the prosecuting attorney Catherine Madder offered the brother a plea bargain that would shorten his jail time if he would testify against his two sisters. The sisters, of course, begged him not to do it. He rejected the offer to protect his family, and the judge sentenced him to thirteen years and eight months in prison.

His decision didn't keep each sister safe. The one who stabbed me in the chest went to trial and was also found guilty. Her prison sentence was seven years, eight months. Later I learned that she gave birth to a baby while in prison. So either she was pregnant when she attacked me or became pregnant shortly thereafter.

Sheridan went to trial too. But she arrived with a fabricated tale that was both unbelievable and brilliant: She claimed I had traveled to Los Angeles to exchange diamonds for drugs. The deal went bad, she said, because the drug dealers had brought a diamond expert who concluded that my merchandise wasn't real but rather cubic zirconia stones that are synthetic gemstones. Infuriated, the drug dealers stabbed me. The jury found her innocent.

By this time, I was suffering so badly from post-traumatic stress disorder (PTSD) that I couldn't get in an elevator or on an airplane. I couldn't even go to a restaurant or leave my house for other reasons because I so feared another murder attempt.

I don't know how it happened, but a nonprofit group that supported victims of crime contacted me and paid for my psychiatric care and hospital bills. They also paid me compensation of more than $40,000.

Then after that bit of luck, while working in my jewelry store, Nancy called me in a panic saying that she saw Sheridan loitering nearby. That was the last straw. We couldn't take it anymore. We immediately organized a "Going out of business" sale, closed our shop, sold my ranch in Castro Valley, and began looking for a home out of state.

I also changed my name and for years whatever new friends I made knew only my false name. Even now, in 2019, despite taking prescribed PTSD medications, I continue to have bouts of stress and fear.

Every day I look at the scars on my body and I know that God was watching over me. He kept me safe.

UGLY DIVORCE

Donna and I married in 1984 at the Bonnie Doone estate that I acquired from my father. Thank God we had agreed on a prenuptial agreement that she signed the day of the wedding before we said, "I do."

In 1989 I had a horrible accident while racing a SuperKart at Portland International Speedway. While I was in the hospital, Donna called to inform me that she was leaving me.

To expedite matters, Donna had come up with the basics of a marital settlement that I agreed to. The marital settlement was mediated by a mutual friend, but Donna's attorney would need to write it up. He never did, and I soon understood why.

Even though I had given Donna everything she had asked for, she decided to take me to court as if we'd never had a property settlement of any kind. The divorce proceedings would take six years to resolve, and Donna would burn through six attorneys, five of whom quit when they figured out she was lying. We also stood before four judges, one of whom announced that he would leave family court because he was tired of seeing everybody at the worst and return to criminal cases where everybody was at their best.

The terms I'd agreed to were quite generous. Eventually, we both filed for restraining orders that we couldn't be within 100 yards of each other. Donna was working at our men's Italian clothing store which was right next to my jewelry store which meant I couldn't go to work. Ray Snow, my attorney, told me to have her fired immediately and I sent over a friend to give her walking papers.

At one point, I got a phone call from one of my employees late one night, Mary, who indicated that Donna was going to commit suicide and was drunk as a skunk. I drove to Donna's condo, which I had given her the down payment to buy. Mary wanted me to spend the night to make sure Donna did not harm herself. There was no way I would've done that.

Donna was lying on the floor, so drunk that she couldn't even stand up. I carried her upstairs and put her in her bed. Then I roamed the house until I found all of her drugs and removed them. I picked up Taryn and Tawny that night, horrified that they would see their mother in that condition, and drove them back to Nancy's house where they would be safe. I should've called the police department and requested that Donna be put on a 5150 suicide watch, a California law that allows a qualified cop or clinician to confine anyone who might be ready to hurt themself.

Donna showed up in court the next day wearing sunglasses in an attempt to hide the major hangover she was suffering. Judge Corrigan commented in open court that "(she) wasn't Snow White but looked more like she was pea green."

On another occasion, Donna went to pick up Taryn after a horse-riding lesson at Eagle Nest Ranch. A friend who was at the stables at the time remarked, "Donna looked like she had been rode hard and put away wet." Later, when I repeated that comment to Donna, she slapped me in the face in front of Taryn, who was five at the time.

My attorney Ray Snow filed a complaint in court and Donna was given ten days community service picking up garbage along the highway. However, her attorney went to the judge and said that she was allergic to the sun, another lie, because she spent time suntanning. The judge did change his ruling after she'd picked up garbage along the highway a few days and let her off the hook, and she was allowed to do the balance of her community service in an office.

In an adorable show of support, one day Taryn presented me with a bank check in the amount of $1,000,000, scrawled in her little-girl handwriting. She'd found Donna's checkbook and decided I deserved a payout. At another time she'd found her mother's gold coins in her shoes and handed me one. I was amused, but made her put it back.

More self-destructive behavior followed. While dining with an aunt and uncle, Donna called me and asked if I would join them for a talk. When I arrived, she was so drunk she was crawling on the floor to get to the bathroom. Believe it or not, the purpose of the meeting was to try to get me to take her back. That's why she'd called in reinforcements for support. By then, there was no chance of rescuing our marriage, with or without members of her extended family. Donna ended up hiring an attorney in Oakland. Wagoner, who was her last attorney, told the judge Corrigan that she had walked out of my house with only two suitcases which was an absolute lie.

Desperate, Donna's attorney Lydia, who worked for Wagoner, put my bookkeeper on the witness stand. Lydia interrogated my bookkeeper Marcia about charges on a company credit card. The expense was for a visit to Marriott's Great America, an amusement park. The attorney was trying to indicate that I had abused my business credit card for personal use. My bookkeeper explained to the court that the expense was for a company party that included my entire staff.

Frustrated that her line of inquiry was getting her nowhere, Lydia said to the judge, "I can't seem to find any evidence."

Judge Corrigan responded, "Maybe there's no evidence to get."

Next, the judge was given a list of things that I had loaned Donna to put in her new condo, which included some furniture. Recalling that Donna had claimed she had left the marriage with only two suitcases, the judge said, "I don't see how all of these items could've been put into two suitcases."

After six years in court Donna's attorneys' fees totaled $650,000 of which $400,000 was owed to her last lawyer who had taken the case because she had convinced him that I would end up paying all legal fees. To avoid the lawyer's invoice, Donna filed for bankruptcy.

This same attorney had spent almost $17,000 in photocopying services to copy all my financial records for my corporation in the diamond business. My attorney Ray Snow said, "Aly, if you want to get this over with, pay the Kinko copying cost and it's done."

The next week I called her attorney's office to say I'd pay the fee but wanted to do it in person. That's fine, the receptionist said.

I went to Wells Fargo and asked them for almost $17,000 in quarters, but they refused to accommodate me. Instead, they offered me one-dollar bills. Done deal.

I took the bag with almost $17,000 one-dollar bills to the lawyer's office. When I arrived, the receptionist indicated that the attorney was with another client. "He'll be with you shortly."

She invited me to wait in a conference room, where I dumped the money on the big meeting table. When the man finally joined me and saw the stack of bills, he said, "I cannot accept cash."

"Okay," I said. "Let's call Judge Corrigan and tell her you don't want to get paid in cash."

He immediately responded, "That's okay. I'll take the cash."

Yet when we had to go to court a final time, he complained that I'd paid him in one-dollar bills, and I was three dollars short.

I loved the judge's retort. She said, "Count it again."

Donna was only awarded $500 per month in child support for both of our daughters, reduced from the $1,500 per month that was in the original agreement. She thought she was going to receive thousands in monthly child support, but now that she was only getting $500 per month, she decided to give the girls to Nancy and me to raise in Idaho.

Taryn and Tawny moved in with us in early 1995 and in December 1995 Tawny moved back to live with her mother. In 1996 Donna took us to court to get both girls back because her aunt and uncle Joan and Edward put pressure on her. They were angry that she gave them up to begin with. After all, they'd put up the money for attorney fees. They even called Nancy several times, yelling and blaming her for taking the girls from Donna. In the end, the court awarded Donna custody, which broke my heart and Nancy's as well.

While in California, Taryn would call Nancy every day when she got home from school to tell her about her day. She was only nine years old and was often left alone. One day she called crying that she was by herself and there was no water. Taryn was not worried about herself; she was worried that she couldn't water the horses. Nancy called the Contra Costa Sheriff Department to do a welfare check. When the deputy arrived, Donna was just pulling into the driveway. Boy, was she mad. Taryn lost her phone privileges as a result. After a year of living with Donna, she moved back in with us.

During the divorce, Donna and I both had restraining orders that forbade us to be within 100 yards of each other. I was having an auction on my front lawn to liquidate merchandise from my store and antiques that belonged to my corporation. I bought a full-page ad in the newspaper saying "Divorce Forces Sale."

I also had shirts made for everyone who helped me at the auction that said, "Ditch the Bitch and Switch." Nancy wore a special shirt that said, "I'm the Switch."

In the middle of the auction Donna showed up, followed by several sheriff cars. She tried to stop the auction, alleging that everything was community property. I told the sheriff in charge to leave my property immediately or I would sue the Sheriff's Department because I could prove that everything belonged to my corporation and Donna had no right to stop the auction.

I also pointed out that I had filed a restraining order.

"FYI, Donna is not allowed within 100 yards of me so she's breaking law. Why don't you arrest her?"

The Sheriff in charge immediately left my property with all of his deputies. If only the divorce had worked that smoothly.

DIAMONDS FROM HEAVEN

Children love balloons filled with helium. Part of the magic is wondering where they would go if they ever got away and rose into the sky and disappeared.

For a party I hosted, I'd inflated at least 200 red and white balloons with helium and then divided them into two groups. They looked great and literally lifted the spirits—even for the adults (kids at heart).

At the end of the party I decided to release them so that we could all watch them float away. But before I let them go, I attached a $1,000 gift certificate to the bottom of each flock of balloons. It was a bit of a stunt, because the certificates could only be claimed at my jewelry store. Another part of me—the fun-loving kid with wonder in his eyes— just wanted to know how far they might travel beyond our spot in Pleasanton, California, and if they would be found.

To my surprise, the air currents swept both balloon bouquets all the way to Wyoming. Both were found by residents who called me to redeem their prizes. One man requested earrings for his wife. That was nice.

I also received calls from newspaper reporters who wrote features about the mysterious balloons in the sky. They wanted to know how my balloons got loose, and when I confessed that it was my idea to set them free, they wanted to know why. I guess I could have answered, "Weren't you ever a kid?"

As it turned out I was lucky my little caper didn't get me in trouble with the Federal Aviation Administration. It is against the law to obstruct the airways because even thin rubber balloons at high altitudes might get sucked into the engines of airplanes and cause them to crash.

Even so, my party favors remind me of the author Linda Poindexter who wrote, "Life is like a balloon. If you never let yourself go, you'll never know how far you can rise."

THE LITTLE BRAT GOT ME GOOD

In the spring of 2018, my daughter Taryn called me from Arizona. She spends a couple months or more down there each year because there is less rain than in California and she loves to compete in barrel races. It's a common and entertaining rodeo event in which a talented rider and horse ride through a cloverleaf course of preset barrels vying for the fastest time. On the phone she got right to the point.

"Dad, I want to borrow some money."

"Oh yeah? How much and what for?"

"I need $50,000 to buy a horse." She sounded excited.

"Why do you want a horse? You've got six or seven of them as it is."

I didn't have to remind her that there was no way she would be able to pay me back from rodeo winnings and other activities. But I talked to Nancy anyway, and we agreed to just give her the horse as a gift.

On our next phone chat, I advised Taryn to go to a Wells Fargo branch and get the wiring instructions. "Then call me back and I'll wire you the money today."

She called with the wiring instructions and as soon as I wrote them down, she was galloping after a new plan.

"Dad, I don't want that horse. There's a better one available."

Curious, I said, "Tell me about it and how much will it cost us?"

Since I love value purchases, even I got excited when I learned the pedigree of this second horse. Pay Cash for Gold was related to a long line of excellent and famous horses, including Dash for Cash, Special Effort, which sold for $1 million as a two-year-old, Strawfly Special, 99 Goldmine, and Judge Cash. All that was very impressive, but I also had to assume the asking price would easily climb to more than $150,000.

"Sorry, Honey, there's no way I'm going to pay more than $50,000. Nancy and I have talked. That's our limit."

She giggled and continued to pitch what she called a "really good deal." When I pressed her for the price tag, she ignored me and just kept talking about the opportunity. "The owners really like me, Dad, and they want me to have it."

"Okay, Taryn, but how much is the horse, dammit?"

More giggles followed and she repeated—*It's a really good deal.*

Now I was getting angry. Was she playing me? She'd kept me hanging on the phone for over ten minutes without telling me the price. Once again, I cursed—"Dammit, just give me the price. You're pissing me off!"

The giggles exploded into waves of laughter at my impatient outburst.

"Taryn! Just tell me the—"

"Dad, it's $15,500. Can you handle that?"

"What? How could it be less than the first horse you wanted?"

"I told you, Dad, the owners like me and the way I race. And they know I don't have a lot of money. So don't look a gift horse in mouth, 'kay?"

She got me good, the little brat, and I could have strangled her for putting me through all that torment. Nancy and I would avoid buying a lesser horse, save $34,500 and yet acquire a much better horse for the barrel racer in our family. Done deal.

Taryn the Tomboy

Taryn's confidence and interests were evident at a very young age. At two years old, she went missing from our home in Bonny Doon, California. Her mother Donna and I were frantic. An exterior kitchen door was open, but we found it difficult to believe that our little girl would have been able to walk or crawl down the steps. And if she had, there were other obstacles awaiting her, including three fences.

We were relieved when our neighbor called to say he had found Taryn and asked us to come over to his barn. This too astounded us because the barn was about 200 yards away from our home. Somehow, our little girl had walked a long distance, while passing several fences and crawling through a small paddock area that lead to a stall inside the barn. That's where we found Taryn.

"She's a horse lover, I guess, right?" Our neighbor chuckled.

Taryn had cuddled up next to a stallion that was lying down on a bed of cedar shavings. Her beautiful head rested on the neck of the glistening steed. Both horse and child seemed perfectly at peace.

Some years later it was clear that Taryn had grown into a tomboy. She loved the great outdoors and explored it freely.

She'd take a bucket to Palomares Creek which was right behind our farmhouse and catch salamanders. One day she returned to our house barefoot and covered in mud, happy as could be, and unafraid of her collection of slithery creatures.

"Dad, look what I got!"

Her curiosity and love for the natural world had its consequences. Taryn was stealing the show and her classroom teacher was unable to get the kids to focus on their studies. By then, I was with Nancy who received a call at my jewelry store from the principal's office. "You have to come get the blue belly lizard away from Taryn. The kids love it and aren't paying attention to the teacher."

Taryn's fearlessness was on full display after we made the move to Idaho. She was only twelve and in the sixth grade the day a boy on the school bus touched her inappropriately. She didn't cower. She clenched her fist and hit him one time in the belly, which made him cry in front of all the other kids. Her reputation spread and the boys got the message: Don't mess with Taryn or she'll make you cry. Even so, there was a reprimand from the principal, who told us the rules dictated that he suspend Taryn for a few days. He also confided that the bully got what he deserved, and said, "I hope my own daughter would respond in the same way."

Not Good but Great

A year after Taryn purchased her prized horse, a friend and trainer Judy Myllymaki took notice. She had taught Taryn how to barrel race in Montana. As a teenager, my daughter would spend a couple months each year learning the skills while also helping Judy train her horses and get them in shape for the racing season.

By 2019 it was apparent that Pay Cash for Gold was unique, so Judy approached Taryn and offered to buy the horse as they prepared for competition in Arizona.

"Congratulations on acquiring Pay Cash for Gold, Taryn. Would you consider selling at a fair price?" Judy asked.

Taryn couldn't understand Judy's need for another horse. "But, Judy, why? You've got several horses you are training, as it is."

"Yes. Those are good horses. But Pay Cash for Gold is a great horse. In a couple years it could take you to the National Finals Rodeo."

Taryn grinned. Making it to the top had always been her goal, and for good reason. She would be competing with the best of the best because the prize money for the NFR barrel racing is so generous.

Judy knew Pay Cash for Gold was an exceptional horse because she understood what type of horse was needed to win the big competitions. Her daughter Rachel Myllymaki had been to the NFR seven times and enjoyed career earnings of over $700,000. At eleven years old, Rachel was the youngest gal to ever make it to the barrel racing finals. At the age of forty-two, she was still in the saddle. She was one of Taryn's best friends and she had helped train the steed. After Taryn allowed her to compete in a few races with Pay Cash for Gold, Rachel said, "I would scrub floors to get this horse!"

If Taryn and Rachel seem mature for such a challenging sport, they are inspired by some great veterans. Mary Burger, an American professional racer, won the World Barrel Racing Championship twice. She took first prize in 2016 at the age of sixty-eight years young. In 2017, she was inducted into the National Cowgirl Museum and Hall of Fame.

I'm proud of Taryn, who at thirty-four has a lot of good riding years ahead of her. While training, she keeps her eye on qualifying for the NFR and hopefully the American Rodeo as well. Both offer a lot of incentive—$1 million prizes for first place.

HOW I GOT OUT OF A SPEEDING TICKET

It was late at night, pitch black, and I was tired because we had been driving cross-country all day from the Castro Valley in California to Challis, Idaho, where we had purchased more than ten acres on the Salmon River. I knew the trip would take at least twelve hours, but that was just fine with me because our new home was paradise.

My passengers were Nancy and my two daughters Taryn and Tawny. Somehow, we also made space for Remington, our French Briard Sheepdog, who occupied the back end of the car.

The interior of my Suburban SUV was quiet and peaceful at that hour as we sped along the near-empty highway. I had a lot to be thankful for, despite my fatigue. Then I saw flashing lights and I was wide awake.

A Sheriff's vehicle was coming toward us fast. This was no surprise because I was flying at 87 miles per hour in a zone with a limit of 65. Nancy and the kids all expressed a version of *uh-oh* when they too noticed law enforcement coming from the other direction and had to turn around to start chasing us. That made me smile.

"Watch this," I told them. "I'm going to get out of this ticket."

After pulling to the side of the highway and stopping, I watched through my side-view mirror as the sheriff got out of his car and approached with his ticket notepad. At the same time, I pushed a button that lowered the rear window so that the cop would be greeted by our ambassador—the very friendly Remington. If that beautiful dog couldn't soften your heart you don't have a heart.

The girls in the back seat watched as their dog poked his big head out the window and whimpered a bit with excitement. Oh boy, a new friend. The sheriff smiled and petted Remington—who could resist?— and then Man's Best Friend reached forward with his big wet sloppy tongue and licked the officer's face. Taryn and Tawny giggled.

When the sheriff came around the side, I rolled down my window.

"What's the hurry, sir?" he asked. "Radar shows you're traveling at 87 miles per hour."

I wish I'd had pictures of our acreage in Challis to show him. I wish I could have explained about the rainbow we all experienced, arcing over our car after a rainstorm, before our first visit to paradise a couple months before. Instead, I kept the explanation short.

"We just bought a place in Challis and I've won a lot of trophies as a race car driver, so going 87 miles per hour is kind of normal for me. Easy to handle."

The sheriff was very amused. He chuckled and shook his head. I doubt he'd ever heard that kind of excuse before.

"All right, sir. Tell you what, I'll let you go this time because you're new to the area. Welcome, by the way. However, please take it easy and *please* drive the speed limit, okay?"

I thanked him as he turned to go. Then he stopped.

"Oh, one more thing."

Uh oh. Now what, I thought.

"Sweet dog."

As we picked up speed on the highway, Nancy and the kids were amazed by what had just transpired. Remington seemed pleased too. In the rear-view mirror I could see his big smile as he panted with joy.

JESUS IS MY SAVIOR

I was baptized at nine years old in the first Baptist Church in Pleasanton, California. It may not have happened if not for Joni, my stepmother, who loved the Lord and convinced me of the importance of attending church every Sunday. Maybe if she had lived longer, I would not have strayed from the church when I was an adult. Joni's death by cancer at the age of forty-four tore me up. After attending her funeral, I swore I would never attend another one. I was twenty-four years old then.

Not long after that personal loss, my diamond business grew, and I enjoyed contributing to various charities and community events. My generosity was extended to a church I had joined with my first wife Susan. But I wasn't always pleased with how things went.

When my pastor announced that the church would like to build a playground for the kids in the congregation, I stepped up and offered to pay the entire cost of $8,000. I've always had a soft spot for children.

"Just bring me the construction invoice," I told the church leaders. "Let's get this done."

Weeks later when the pastor came to my business office and handed me a bill for about $17,000, I was puzzled.

"What's this?"

"You said you'd make a charitable donation to pay for the playground," my pastor said.

"But this is more than double the amount I agreed to pay." The truth was, at that moment, I didn't have the cash flow to handle the unexpected price hike. And no one had come to me to discuss it. "What happened?"

"Well, Aly, I know you're a big success in the diamond trade, so when I was given the chance to create a more expensive playground that would better serve our kids, I assumed you could afford it."

That annoyed me. It felt like I was being taken advantage of. My temper flared.

"Get out!"

The pastor was stunned. "What?"

"I said, 'Get out.'"

"But—"

"But nothing. Get out and don't let the door hit you in the ass because I don't want to get sued."

My gripe expanded a few years later. By then, I'd begun using cocaine, though Susan and I were still church members. In fact, we relied on our community for counseling when our marriage hit troubled waters. We saw one counselor on a regular basis, and I believed we were making progress. Then the woman made an announcement.

"We can't counsel you anymore," she said.

"Why?" I asked.

The answer to my question came when I learned the counselor had suggested that Susan divorce me.

I really can't understand why she would do that. "Isn't the church supposed to help us, not kick us out?"

"We're not asking Susan to leave."

Well, if they didn't want me, I reasoned, then I didn't want or need them. I stopped attending services and sometimes wondered what Joni might have said, if she were still alive. But she wasn't. And maybe, deep down, I blamed the church for that too. So I strayed.

Despite my exit from religious life, the Lord Jesus never left me. I know now He was still looking over me because I survived the nine lives of a cat.

After my move to Idaho with Nancy and my daughters Taryn and Tawny, I'd already had two knee operations when I fell and blew out my right knee again. The pain and frustration were enormous. I didn't know how I could endure it. Then I got an idea.

I called a friend who was a member of the church in Challis I'd joined.

"Do you believe in the power of God to heal?"

"Yes, Aly, I do. It says so in the Bible."

Then I asked if he had any personal knowledge of anyone who had truly been healed through prayer.

"Well ... " He hemmed and hawed and I knew what was coming next. "No, I can't say that I have any personal knowledge of that kind."

My reply surprised him. "I'm in excruciating pain. Would you come over to the house and pray with me? I need help asking God to heal my knee, and I don't know where else to turn."

When he arrived, my friend put his hands on my knee, and we prayed for God to heal me. Heal me now, Lord. I can't take this anymore.

The pain disappeared instantly. After the healing, this is what I wrote:

Aly Bruner

Life Without Jesus is a Life Not Worth Living

So long, I've been looking too hard
I've been waiting so long

Sometimes I don't know what I will find,
I only know it's a matter of time

When you've found Jesus,

When you've found your Savior

It feels so right so warm and true
I need to know if you feel it too

Without Jesus you are lost without him

Won't you tell me if I'm coming on too strong?
I don't want to scare you away from knowing our Lord
and Savior.

This heart of mine has been hurt before,
This time I know I am sure

I've been waiting for a Savior who
Who came into my life

I've been waiting — for someone to
to make me feel alive

Yeah, waiting

Because he made the sacrifice
To die on Calvary
Our salvation will survive. So now I feel alive
He's so good, it's understood
More than a touch or a word we say
It's not just my dreams, that it feels this way

When you love Jesus

Yeah, really love Jesus

Now I know it's right
From the moment I wake up 'til deep in the night
There's nowhere on earth that I'd rather be,
Hand in hand with him, tenderly

I've been waiting,
for something whole, to make me feel alive

So now I know I know my friend, that
A Life Without Jesus is a Life Not Worth Living

With a broken body and a dear friend
We prayed together, Dear Lord, My body to mend
It is through faith, not prayer alone
He made me whole so I picked up the phone
It is my need, to tell the world

Aly Bruner

Now I know, I know he's real
It's through faith and prayer, he did heal

Now that he's come back into my life
Can't you see the change in me!

I know that there will be no more sorrow, because tonight
I'm going to love him like there will be no tomorrow

RAINBOWS END RECOVERY CENTER

In 2011 Nancy and I decided to help men and women with their addictions after witnessing the suffering some recovering family members and friends went through. My own alcohol-driven foolishness also played a role in our new project.

In 2009 after Nancy and I had been married for a decade, I began to abuse alcohol. At the time, I was suffering from non-diagnosed post-traumatic stress disorder that began after being robbed and stabbed at LAX. My psychiatrist, whom I was seeing weekly, prescribed Ambien, a horrible drug that only added to my problems and made me so paranoid that I began to have panic attacks. One event was so severe—I was sure I was dying—that I had to be air-lifted from our home in Challis by the Life Flight organization at night during a snowstorm. The helicopter landed safely at a hospital in Idaho Falls.

My bouts with heavy intoxication caused me to do some very stupid things. One day when a state Fish and Game officer came to our home to remove a deer that had died after being hit by a car, I jokingly pulled out a Browning 380 pistol and suggested we have target practice. He was tape-recording the conversation when I recklessly added, "This is like a shootout at the O.K. Corral."

My behavior was awful. But, unfortunately, the officer lied and said I pulled the pistol on him. In fact, I unloaded the handgun at his request. If I'd pointed the weapon at him, wouldn't he have arrested me once the ammunition had been removed? His accusation took me to court where I was charged with a felony. When I appeared before the judge, he listened to the tape recording and said that it sounded like I was attempting suicide by cop. In lieu of going to jail, the judge allowed me to enter a rehabilitation program for ninety days. I paid a hefty price, as many alcoholics do, for my addiction. The total cost of rehab plus attorney fees was more than $100,000.

After getting sober and winning praise for my good behavior during the community service phase of my sentence, my probation officer went before the judge and requested that my felony be reduced to a misdemeanor on December 15, 2010, as one of the luckiest days of my life. Thank God the judge approved the change in my record. The stress and remorse I felt made me want to help others get out of the hell created by addiction.

But Nancy and I experienced quite an ordeal when seeking approval to open our recovery center. We had to go before the Challis planning and zoning commissions to request that our property be rezoned. Members of those boards had plenty of questions, and we faced a lot of opposition from neighbors. Even the people in the center of town—miles from our property— were worried. They didn't like the idea of having drug and alcohol addicts in their midst because they feared crime, such as home invasions. A couple of women even mentioned rape.

As it turned out, a federal law stated that it was mandatory for the planning and zoning commissions to approve our application. The city leaders in Idaho City, Boise County, denied an application in 2010 to rezone property for a recovery center that resulted in a lawsuit that the city lost. The applicants were awarded $5 million in damages. But to avoid the hefty payout, the city filed for bankruptcy. The federal law was a way to overcome the age-old curse of NIMBY—Not In My Backyard—that has thwarted many kinds of zoning requests.

We wrangled with commission members for several months before we discovered the federal law and showed the newspaper article to our town leaders. Finally, our application was approved. But just because we had a good cause and the best intentions didn't mean we immediately succeeded.

After five years, Rainbows End Recovery Center was severely in the red. I'd made a lot of money throughout my career by knowing when to hold my cards or fold them. In general, it is better to take a loss early, before things get out of hand. So in 2016, while bleeding money, I had to pop the question.

"Nancy, do you think we should close the center?"

She answered without hesitation. "How do you put a price on saving people's lives?"

I quickly reversed the trend of financial loss by improving our marketing program with television advertisements. By 2018, we were completely out of debt and have remained in the black ever since.

Despite our early struggles with operating costs, the recovery center was selected out of over 100,000 similar businesses to be featured in a behind-the-scenes documentary that was narrated by award-winning actor James Earl Jones. We were visited by a camera crew, which interviewed Nancy and staff members, and we were given an incredible seven-minute video that was aired nationally and is now featured on our website.

We are licensed by the state of Idaho, and proud to be Joint Commission certified, which is recognized nationwide as a symbol of quality services and standards. We also have credentials for helping war veterans who suffer from post-traumatic stress disorder. It is very sad that on average twenty-two war vets commit suicide each day. That's over 8,000 per year.

Our facility has fourteen beds, but we typically help only six to eight clients at a time, and occasionally as many as eleven. Our success rate is a phenomenal 70 percent, which outperforms nationwide rehabilitation statistics that indicate only 10 percent of alcoholics stay sober, and only 5 percent of heroin meth addicts stay clean. Since our opening, we've helped hundreds of people overcome debilitating addictions and lead wonderful lives. Nancy made the right choice to keep the recovery center open.

ACKNOWLEDGEMENTS

My deepest gratitude to the many people who have supported me through the years. Especially my friend Eddie Tompkins who is almost as crazy as I am. My loving wife Nancy who has stuck by my side through thick and thin. My father Alston who taught me that your word is your bond. The real treasure in life is family and friends. I love you all.

Thanks to Douglas Glenn Clark for his writing and publishing consultations. His guidance was excellent. https://www.your-ghost-writer.com/

ABOUT THE AUTHOR

Aly Bruner found fame and fortune as a diamond importer, jewelry designer and manufacturer. He is also an entrepreneur, world traveler, thrill seeker, art lover, champion race car driver, treasure hunter and an artist. His specialty is bronze sculptures that were inspired by the workers and musicians he observed during his childhood in North Carolina. His work has been featured in galleries worldwide. In 2011, Bruner and his wife Nancy Del Colletti, founded a co-ed dual-diagnosis facility that provides treatment for people suffering from drug and/or alcohol and co-occurring psychological conditions. https://www.rainbowsendrecoverycenter.com/

CPSIA information can be obtained
at www.ICGtesting.com
Printed in the USA
FSHW020123060920
73574FS

9 780578 673691